Victims

of

Convention

Victims
of
Convention

BY
J E A N E . K E N N A R D

ARCHON BOOKS
Hamden, Connecticut
1978

© Jean E. Kennard 1978
First published 1978 as an Archon Book,
an imprint of The Shoe String Press, Inc.,
Hamden, Connecticut 06514

Library of Congress Cataloging Publication Data

Kennard, Jean E.   1936-
Victims of convention.

Bibliography: p.
Includes index.
1. English fiction—19th century—History and criticism.
2. Women in literature. 3. Courtship in literature.
I. Title.
PR830.W6K4   823'.085   77-17194
ISBN 0-208-01659-7

For my parents, in gratitude for
an upbringing that included Victorian novels

Contents

	Introduction	9
Chapter One	Jane Austen: The Establishment	21
Chapter Two	Aristrocrat versus Commoner	46
Chapter Three	Capital Punishment	63
Chapter Four	A Question of Mastery: The Novels of Charlotte Brontë	80
Chapter Five	A Wife Who Waddles: The Novels of George Eliot	108
Chapter Six	Her Transitory Self	136
	Conclusion	158
	Notes	168
	Selected Bibliography	181
	Index	193

Introduction

THE NINETEENTH CENTURY was the period that produced the great British women novelists,—Jane Austen, The Brontës, George Eliot,—and coined such terms as "the new woman" and "the woman question." It is an obvious period to attract feminist investigation. Since the publication in 1970 of Kate Millett's *Sexual Politics* feminist critics have, indeed, turned their attention increasingly to the Victorian novel. Although books on the subject of women in nineteenth-century fiction predate *Sexual Politics*—Patricia Thomson's *The Victorian Heroine* (1956) and Hazel Mews's *Frail Vessels* (1969), for example—Millett's brief discussion of *Villette*, *The Egoist*, and *Jude the Obscure* undoubtedly marks a turning point. It is impossible to write on the subject now and ignore the fact that this has been claimed as feminist territory, although the books that have appeared since 1970 represent a variety of approaches, not all of them avowedly feminist. Some, like Elizabeth Hardwick's *Seduction and Betrayal* (1974) and Patricia Beer's *Reader, I Married Him* (1974), are feminist only in the limited sense that they discuss female writers and characters. Vineta Colby's *Yesterday's Woman* (1974) is a discussion of the literary techniques of domestic realism in the first half of the century. Others cover a greater range of material in an attempt to trace sociological or psychological truths about women and women writers. Jenni Calder's *Women and Marriage in Victorian Fiction* (1976), Patricia Meyer Spacks's *The Female Imagination* (1975) and Ellen

Moers's *Literary Women* (1976) are typical of these. New books are promised: Elaine Showalter's *A Literature of Their Own* comes out this year.

It is reasonable to question, then, whether we really need another book in this field at all. Is there anything, in fact, that these studies have not covered? I think there is. Except perhaps for Moers's *Literary Women* and Françoise Basch's *Relative Creatures* (1974), few of these books have made a clear distinction between fictional formula and historical or social truth. This seems to me a serious problem in current feminist criticism generally: the tendency to treat literature, particularly the novel, as mimetic in the simplest way, as the documentation, more or less accurate, of certain human experiences. This tendency is illustrated, for example, by Patricia Meyer Spacks's labeling fiction a "concealed form of autobiography."[1] It is a danger for those primarily interested in social history as well as for literary critics, for only when we clearly identify the literary conventions which influenced fiction can we separate these from any sociological truths the novels may illustrate.

The premise behind my argument is that novelists read as well as live in society. This is obvious enough in the case of the Victorian novelists whose libraries and reading habits are known to us. Yet all too often we write about their work as if they were imitating life and had no conception of fictional form to both aid and hinder their creativity.[2] Certainly the relationship between the influence of social conditions and that of literature is a complex one, and presumably differs with individual writers, but it serves no purpose to ignore the effect of a literary tradition.

In particular, feminist critics have scarcely started to investigate the sexism implicit in certain fictional structures. This area is potentially a large one and is related to the even broader question of feminism as style.[3] What I have attempted here is, I imagine, merely a beginning: the demonstration of the fundamentally sexist nature of one dominant structural convention in Victorian novels with central female characters.

I have called this convention the convention of the two

suitors, and this book is a study of its use in nineteenth-century British fiction, though it continues to be used, in a changed form, even in contemporary fiction. My aim is partly identification: to demonstrate the frequency of the convention's appearance and to illustrate the variety of its modes. The most interesting aspect of the subject, though, is a conflict between the convention and the more modern concept of female maturity that develops during the nineteenth century. This conflict frequently creates difficulties in even the greatest Victorian novels. Once recognized, it often provides a clearer explanation for problems critics have already noted and which, in some instances, have become part of the staple diet of critical debate: the marriage of Will Ladislaw to Dorothea Brooke in *Middlemarch,* for example, or the injuries to Rochester in *Jane Eyre.*

I have chosen the novels discussed in this study either because they are important in themselves or because they illustrate particular variations on the convention, but there are others which might have served as well. I realize that the great Victorian novels are much more than illustrations of a convention based on the binary opposition of two suitors, but they are also this, a fact which has not until now been recognized.

The form in which the convention of the two suitors dominates Victorian fiction was firmly established by Jane Austen.[4] She adapted the formula of the female quixotic novel, in which a young girl learns to abandon a view of the world based on fantasy and adjust herself to reality, and incorporated in it certain characters from the novel of sensibility.[5] She used two of them in particular, the unscrupulous or "wrong" suitor and the exemplary or "right" suitor, as touchstones of value in her heroine's progress towards maturity. The growth of a woman in a Jane Austen novel is marked by her choice of the right suitor over the wrong suitor. The wrong suitor embodies the qualities she must reject; the right suitor those which, in Jane Austen's view, make for the good life. The heroine's personality and development are thus defined through comparison with two male characters.

This pattern occurs in minor novels which precede Jane

Austen's, most typically in a parody of the novel of sensibility, Charlotte Lennox's *The Female Quixote* (1752) which appears to have been a major influence on *Northanger Abbey.* In *The Female Quixote,* the heroine Arabella has been so influenced by French romances that she imagines them to be an authentic portrayal of life. She has two suitors: Charles Glanville, a realist, and Sir George Bellmour who, in order to succeed with Arabella, makes the great mistake of pretending to agree with her female vision of the world. Arabella's maturing lies in seeing through the false Sir George and in recognizing the value of Charles Glanville's good sense, a creditable achievement considering that she suffers to an unusual degree the handicaps of her successors, isolation from any experience outside the drawing room and a lack of serious education. Maturity is seen to consist of adjusting oneself to the real world which is synonymous with becoming like the right suitor. The attainment of maturity wins the great reward, marriage to the right suitor, which provides a conclusion to the novel.

Although it is usually more heavily fleshed than in *The Female Quixote,* a similar skeleton exists in numerous other novels: Jane Austen's Elizabeth Bennet must recognize the weakness of Wickham and the virtues of Darcy; Emma the shallowness of Frank Churchill and the true worth of George Knightley. George Eliot's Dorothea Brooke must exchange the sterility of Casaubon for the warmth of Will Ladislaw. In George Meredith's *The Egoist,* Clara Middleton has to reject the egotism of Willoughby for the sensitivity of Vernon Whitford.

The convention of the two suitors exists in some form in almost every novel with a central female character, particularly if the term *suitor* is used loosely, as I use it, to refer to those men who are seen by the author as potential mates for the heroine, even if she never considers them seriously or if they never have any intention of proposing marriage. Thus in *Northanger Abbey,* John Thorpe is a suitor to Catherine Morland even though she finds him merely irritating and has no intention of accepting his proposal; George Eliot's Daniel Deronda functions as a suitor to Gwendolen Harleth even though he never intends to propose to her. Each of these men represents one pole of value in the novel in which he appears and each is deliberately contrasted to another man who eventually marries the heroine.

As I shall demonstrate in chapter one, the two suitors convention works well for Jane Austen, in spite of her spirited heroines who are often subordinated in marriage to less interesting heroes, because there is really no conflict between these marriages and Austen's ideology. In Augustan fashion she argues for some submission to the social order for all her characters, men as well as women.

The convention also works well when the maturing of the heroine is not the primary focus of the novel, even though she may be its central character. She may function as a sort of docile everywoman who acquires certain qualities as she learns the worth of the right suitor but she never really absorbs our interest. In chapter two I shall discuss four novels of this kind: Mrs. Gaskell's *Mary Barton;* Anthony Trollope's *Dr. Thorne;* Wilkie Collins's *The Woman in White* and George Eliot's *Felix Holt.* In each the choice between vice and virtue is indeed a choice between two suitors, but the moral interest lies in the opposing ways of life they represent rather than in the person who makes the choice. The authors of these novels avoid the major difficulty with the convention, a conflict between our response to the conventions of romantic comedy and our involvement in a psychologically realistic presentation of a complex heroine.

In certain novels the convention may work satisfactorily even though the heroine is a complex individual. If she makes the wrong choice early on, as in *Wuthering Heights* or in the Hardy novels discussed in chapter three, the convention creates no problems because we are never asked to accept the woman's reaching some independent maturity. She merely has to die for her mistake.

The convention creates problems only when the heroine's development is central to the novel and when, at its end, she supposedly achieves a form of maturity which involves the modern virtues of independence and individuality. This is variously defined in the novels but is centered in the notions of freedom and self-fulfillment. Since in order to reach maturity the heroine must accept certain values and since the repository of those values is, according to the convention, the right suitor, at the end of the novel she invariably appears to have subordinated her own personality to that of the hero. The convention tends, therefore, to imply that the good man,—who, after all, held the virtues first,—is superior to the woman who can, with some effort, be taught to emulate him. The very structure of the novel places him as leader, her as follower. For her, maturity lies in learning that her ideals are fantasies, that happiness lies in approximating the male reality and in denying much of what had seemed to be herself. The structure is, thus, inherently sexist.

Are we as readers really satisfied by the marriage of Dorothea Brooke to Will Ladislaw? of Shirley Keeldar to Louis Moore? of Clara Middleton to Vernon Whitford? Although the endings of *Middlemarch, Shirley,* and *The Egoist* may be, in a superficial sense, aesthetically satisfying, should Dorothea, Shirley and Clara have been satisfied with these marriages? Haven't the qualities we have been invited to admire in these heroines been sacrificed to structural neatness?[6] The satisfaction of the reader is, of course, impossible to measure and will inevitably vary. But large numbers of readers have expressed concern over the implications of these marriages and others have found need to justify them. There seems reason enough to assume a problem.

The concluding marriage may be perceived as unsatisfactory in two ways. The right suitor may seem an inadequate embodiment of the virtues to be emulated by the heroine even though he is obviously intended to embody them. Will Ladislaw and Vernon Whitford are good examples here. Or the right suitor may be idealized, which clarifies but does not resolve the real problem. If he is idealized, he first runs the risk of failing as a fictional character by seeming one-dimensional in contrast to the more complex presentation of the heroine. Second, as an example of virtues achieved prior to the heroine's maturity, the idealized right suitor must, at least implicitly, take on the role of guide or mentor, as, for example, George Knightley does in *Emma.* This, as I explained above, inevitably leaves the heroine in the position of imitator, an obvious conflict with the quality of independence we have been invited to admire in her. At the end of the novel we may therefore be asked to respond postively to two mutually exclusive conclusions: the maturation of the heroine and the completion of the romantic comedy plot.

Although this may seem to suggest that no marriage could be satisfactory for the heroine, which in some instances may be true, the problem with the convention does not necessarily imply this. The problem lies only in the marriage of the heroine to a man who has throughout the novel been used to illustrate the qualities she must acquire; our sense of her mature independence would not necessarily be jeopardized if she were to marry a man who had not functioned in this fashion.

The novels of Charlotte Brontë and George Eliot discussed in chapters four and five have serious structural problems because qualities the reader is invited to admire in the heroine are often inadequately met by her marriage to the right suitor. Both Brontë and Eliot are to some extent victims of the two suitors convention as are certain of their heroines. We also began to see in their novels specific comments on the situation of women, comments which become dominant in the novels discussed in chapter six: *The Egoist, A Room with a View, The Odd Women,* and *Ann Veronica.* When support for female independence is directly expressed by the novelist, the two suitors convention may well break the structural back of the novel altogether.

The problem caused by the convention increases, of course, in proportion to the modernity of the view of female maturity either implied or directly stated in the novel. It would be convenient to suggest that the concept of female maturity became progressively closer to our own as the nineteenth century advanced and thus justify a neat chronological development for my own book. Inconveniently, it is not so. Charlotte Brontë may have written before Trollope but her modern view of female maturity causes structural problems in her novels that he avoids by clinging to an older notion of women. Therefore I have abandoned a chronological scheme and simply discuss first those instances where the convention works well, leaving until the second half of the book the problems caused by the convention.

There is an obvious argument against considering the marriage of heroine to hero in a novel as merely a convention. Certainly there were, for various reasons, few avenues except marriage open to the nineteenth-century woman.[7] Throughout the century some female novelists stressed the imporatance of a woman's earning her own living and argued bitterly against society's refusal to let her do so. Charlotte Brontë's complaint in *Shirley* (1848) that women have no employment but housework, sewing, visiting, and dressing to ensnare husbands has numerous echoes. But the complaints were not limited to novels nor to women. In *Blackwoods* for July 1857, for example, a writer of an article on Charlotte Brontë pointed out that her life was an illustration of "what hundreds of young women have to undergo who have no proper outlet for their mental activities. . . . They can become either governesses or authoresses."

Charlotte Brontë was talented enough to be both teacher and writer, but most women, of course, were not. The chief alternative to marriage for the semieducated middle-class girl was work as a governess,[8] but the conditions of this employment were such that Gwendolen Harleth's decision to marry even a man she disliked rather than pursue it is hardly surprising. Some form of artistic or literary endeavor often provided occupation for women but was not generally regarded as a livelihood. In Charles Reade's *Love Me Little, Love Me Long* (1859), Lucy Fountain explains that an ambitious girl can choose marriage or watercolors and that she has chosen "the altar and not the easel" because it is more fashionable.

The opposition to allowing women to work and thus to providing them with opportunities to do so was justified by the dual notions that women are naturally inferior in all activities except those of the affections and that it is somehow unwomanly for them to attempt anything else. This pernicious doctrine, which colors all nineteenth-century thinking about women, is, of course, best expressed by Ruskin in "Of Queen's Gardens" (1871). Man is "the doer, the creator, the discoverer, the defender," claims Ruskin; woman's intellect is "for sweet ordering, arrangement and decision. . . . She must be enduringly, incorruptibly good; instinctively, infallibly wise—wise, not for self-development, but for self-renuncia- tion. . . . Her great function is Praise."⁹ He hardly has to name the object of her praise. Her functions, qualities and education are defined in terms of man's needs, not her own, and justified under the rubric of chivalry: "You cannot think that the buckling on of the knight's armor by his lady's hand was a mere caprice of romantic fashion. It is the type of an eternal truth."¹⁰

Ruskin's view prevails in nineteenth-century England in spite of being resoundingly defeated at least twice in the previous eighty years. In *A Vindication of the Rights of Women* (1792) Mary Wollstonecraft, arguing for the benefits of equal education for women, points out that women have been "Localized . . . by the rank they are in, by *courtesy*."¹¹ Only two years before Ruskin's lecture, John Stuart Mill's vigorous defense of legal rights for women, *On the Subjection of Women* (1869), states "no one can safely pronounce that if woman's nature were left to choose its direction as freely as man's and if no artificial bent were attempted to be given to it . . . there would be any material difference, or perhaps any difference at all, in the character and capacities which would unfold themselves."¹²

Yet many novelists—and not only male novelists—appear to agree with Ruskin. Mrs. Craik's *Olive* exemplifies the attitude: "no woman can be an artist—that is a great artist. The hierarchies of the soul's dominion belong only to man, and it is right they should. . . . Nature, which gave to man the dominion of the intellect, gave to her that of the heart and affections. . . . there scarcely ever lived the woman who would not rather sit meekly by her own hearth, with her husband at her side, and her children at her knee, than be crowned Corinne of the Capitol."¹³ With all this propaganda it is hardly surprising that given a choice between being a second-rate artist and a wife, most nineteenth-century girls opted for marriage. The inevitability of marriage as the only viable future for the single female may well have been a truth of nineteenth-century life as well as of fiction. Even the greatest supporters of women's rights, Wollstonecraft and Mill, are primarily concerned with women's rights to equality within the bounds of marriage.

However, I am not primarily concerned here with this fact of Victorian life; I am concerned with a literary convention, a method of structuring a work of fiction which implies attitudes but does not, in any direct sense, reflect life. First, it is not the fact that the heroine marries which is significant but that the marriage acts as a conclusion to the novel and is to a large extent symbolic. It indicates the adjustment of the protagonist to society's values, a condition which is equated with her maturity. Its function is literary and structural; a woman's life did not end with marriage even in nineteenth-century England, nor, presumably, was she mature in her early twenties.

Second, the embodiment of vice and virtue in two suitors and the definition of the heroine's character through comparison with them must be a purely literary device with no relationship at all to the realities of courtship in nineteenth-century England. By what coincidence would any woman meet and be courted by a man who exemplified her own weaknesses as the wrong suitor does in the convention? This aspect of the convention provides the answer to those who suggest that the male *bildungsroman* must also be sexist in instances where a male protagonist chooses between two women. A male protagonist, however, is not defined in terms of two women and is invariably also seen in relation to other aspects of life. As Jenni Calder says of David Copperfield, "For all his valuing of Agnes, his Ministering Angel, he sees her all the time as outside the main business of life. . . . Agnes is David's reward for hard work and application, not for a matured understanding of human needs and impulses."[14]

Third, the two suitors convention does not disappear from the novel as opportunities for a different life for women increase. Women are still described in fiction almost exclusively in terms of their relationships with men. Except possibly in the novels of Virginia Woolf or, more recently, in the work of Margaret Laurence and Gail Godwin, few new forms have been developed. It is hard to name a novel in which a woman's sexual life is related to her development as, for instance, Stephen Dedalus's is to his: that is, as an important but not total influence.

In most contemporary novels with a central female character, the two suitors convention has often merely been adapted to a later stage in the heroine's life in a way established by Lawrence in *Lady Chatterley's Lover.* The husband now plays the role of the wrong suitor who represents the stifling world of bourgeois values; the lover is the right suitor who represents freedom and the chance for a richer life.[15] This is the form of the convention Doris Lessing has used for almost every novel in *The Children of Violence* series. Martha Quest, who in *A Proper Marriage* leaves her husband by means of a lover, is still repeating the pattern many years and several novels later in *A Four-Gated City,* a novel which only transcends the problem by means of a visionary science fiction ending.

It is not insignificant that Doris Lessing echoes a complaint George Gissing had made sixty years earlier in *The Odd Women,* a novel very sensitive to the situation of women. In a scene in Gissing's novel an independent woman teacher, Rhoda Nunn, makes the following complaint to her business partner: "If every novelist could be strangled and thrown into the sea we should have some chance of reforming women. . . . What is more vulgar than the ideal of novelists? they won't represent the actual world; it would be too dull for their readers. In real life how many men and women *fall in love?* . . . There is the sexual instinct, of course, but that is quite a different thing; the novelists daren't talk about that. The paltry creatures daren't tell the one truth that would be profitable."[16] In a 1952 novel, *A Proper Marriage,* Lessing's Martha Quest also complains that novelists do not tell the truth: "In the books, the young and idealistic girl gets married, has a baby—she at once turns into something quite different; and she is perfectly happy to spend her whole life bringing up children with a tedious husband."[17] The world had changed for women, not perhaps as much as one would like, but it had changed by 1952. Yet contemporary novelists are in some ways no more honest than those Martha Quest complains of.

They are trapped in a convention—a literary, not a social one—made popular by Jane Austen.

Although the contemporary forms of the two suitors convention are interesting, I have decided against including a thorough examination of them in this book. In discussing *Ann Veronica* and *A Room with a View* I have, of course, ventured into the twentieth century and it is a temptation to continue. But the novel as a form changed so dramatically in the second decade of this century that a consideration of a character's maturing in the nineteenth-century sense is frequently irrelevant to it. One can hardly discuss the maturing of Clarissa Dalloway. It is also, perhaps, significant that there are very few British novels of the twenties, thirties and forties with central female characters. The contemporary reawakening of interest in the situation of women as a subject for fiction has hardly been going long enough to see clearly what changes it may make in the structural conventions of the novel. There are, however, some promising new directions which I shall mention briefly in my final chapter.

Chapter One

Jane Austen:
The Establishment

JANE AUSTEN established the two suitors convention in the tradition of the English novel, transforming structural patterns, stock characters and situations from earlier fiction in such a way that they usually seem uniquely appropriate to her own ideas. For her, the convention works well. In spite of some lapses in its execution in *Sense and Sensibility* and *Mansfield Park,* only once, in *Emma,* is there any suggestion of that basic conflict between the two suitors convention and the notion of female maturity which will appear in the novels of later writers. The success of the convention in Jane Austen's novels is one explanation for its popularity throughout the nineteenth century.

Two undisputed critical commonplaces about Jane Austen are that she stressed the importance of social structure, the limitation of personal impulse by convention, and that her novels are closely related to the fictional conventions of the eighteenth century.[1] A. Walton Litz and Tony Tanner[2] both comment particularly on Jane Austen's tendency to adopt the eighteenth-century prose writers use of antitheses, a tendency which can be seen clearly in the titles of two of her novels: *Sense and Sensibility* and *Pride and Prejudice.* This use of antitheses is closely related to her development of the convention of the two suitors in which the virtues of the right suitor are set against the vices of the wrong suitor.

Each of Jane Austen's six major novels has a heroine (with the exception of *Sense and Sensibility* which has two) who is either attracted to or sought in marriage by two men, one of whom, in general terms, embodies the qualities Jane Austen admires, the other their opposite. The convention is, of course, more subtly used than this oversimplification suggests. There is an attempt to suggest weakness and even in change in some of the right suitors: Darcy and Wentworth, perhaps, learn something. The wrong suitors are not always complete villains: Frank Churchill is even worthy enough to marry the admirable Jane Fairfax. But it is true that the right suitor is to a large extent idealized and that Jane Austen quite deliberately contrasts his qualities with their absence in the wrong suitor. It is also true that by the time the heroine marries the right suitor she has perceived his values to be the correct ones and has adopted them for herself.

The two suitors convention works for Jane Austen because the concept of maturity which she asks her reader to accept for her heroines is not the modern one of the development of the self and the complete independence of personality; Emma, for example, is condemned for being directed chiefly by her own judgment. Jane Austen's idea of the mature female has been variously defined: Dorothy Van Ghent has described this maturity as "emotional intelligence";[3] Kenneth Moler prefers "self-knowledge," which he defines as a balance between judgment and feeling, between "art" and "nature."[4]

The great sins of four of Jane Austen's heroines—Fanny Price and Anne Elliot are virtually sinless—can be described as too great a sensibility, an excess on the side of nature, which is the sin of Catherine Morland and Marianne Dashwood, or too great a self-will, an excess on the side of art which, as in Elizabeth Bennet and Emma Woodhouse, manifests itself as witty intelligence. These sins have something in common: they both result in a failure to perceive reality. Too great a sensibility prevents both Catherine and Marianne from perceiving the true nature of those around them; too great a self-will makes Emma, and to a lesser extent Elizabeth, use other people as puppets in a world of their own making which equally blinds them to the real world. Each of Jane Austen's novels, except *Mansfield Park*, is a novel about perception; maturity for her heroines consists in recognizing the reality of others and in accepting responsibility towards them. In other words, it consists in finding one's rightful place in the social structure. In *Northanger Abbey, Sense and Sensibility, Pride and Prejudice, Emma,* and possibly *Persuasion,* the reality the heroine must perceive and accept is the true nature of the right suitor who has understood the world and to a large extent established his values before she meets him.

The convention of the two suitors is acceptable to us in a Jane Austen novel because she expects all her characters—not just her women—to accept some limitation of their personalities for the sake of the social structure. As Tony Tanner says, " . . . for Jane Austen the structure of society was more powerful than the structure of feeling in any one individual and would always contain it."[5] The right suitor, too, is seen in his role of ideal gentleman as balancing the claims of "art" and "nature." His duty as a member of society can never be sacrificed to personal inclination. Such limitation in the name of the general good is part of the value scheme Jane Austen advocates, though it is important to recognize her careful discrimination between social custom, which can be legitimately rejected when necessary, and the more fundamental bonds of the social contract. The wrong suitor, although often having the appearance of virtue—only John Thorpe does not—is merely superficially charming. He is invariably weak and this weakness takes the form of self-indulgence, of breaking the social code. The right suitor pays the price of living within the social restrictions and gains the heroine as his reward. What is fair for the hero can be accepted as fair for the heroine.

In no instance in a Jane Austen novel are we dissatisfied by the marriage of the heroine to the right suitor because of a failure in the thematic argument. In other words, Jane Austen is completely aware of each quality she mentions in her heroine, understands fully those faults which must be corrected and allows the heroine to understand the need for correcting them herself before she marries the right suitor who, of course, has already reached this insight. There are no qualities or drives which Jane Austen has invited us to admire in the heroine which are irreconcilable with this marriage.

Where we are dissatisfied with the marriage—and in the cases of Marianne Dashwood and Emma Woodhouse some readers perhaps are—it is because we disagree with Jane Austen's values. We cannot reconcile those qualities we have found attractive in the heroine with the qualities of the hero she has now adopted. But the reasons for finding attractive qualities in Marianne or Emma which Jane Austen asks us to disapprove probably lie rather in the modern preferences of the reader than in any failure of execution on the part of Jane Austen.

The major problem with *Northanger Abbey*, the relationship between the work as a satire on the popular Gothic and sensibility novels and its function as a realistic apprenticeship novel of a girl's maturing, is not central to my discussion.[6] However, the fact that this novel is to a large extent satire, and therefore employs exaggeration, is helpful here; it allows the bare bones of the two suitors convention to be seen very clearly. If it were not Jane Austen's first major novel, it would nevertheless be a convenient starting point. Mudrick points out that the characters are strictly functional, that they are antitypes created to reverse or contradict corresponding type characters from the Gothic novels.[7] Jane Austen gives her characters the faults of common life rather than the more sensational vices of Gothic characters in order to illustrate one of her major themes, that "the common feelings of common life"[8] can lead to disasters no less serious than those portrayed in the fiction she parodies. But their relationship to the types they are drawn from is kept constantly before us, and thus they never really escape flatness. Mr. Morland is the tyrannical father figure reversed; Mrs. Allen the neglectful, though never deliberately vicious, chaperone.

Catherine is introduced as an antitype also—the antitype of the Gothic heroine—and although she partially escapes the satirical treatment, its initial use prevents her from ever becoming interesting or complex in her own right. *Northanger Abbey* could therefore have been discussed equally well with the flat-heroine novels of chapter two. Catherine's lack of complexity can be explained in terms of the way Jane Austen introduces and develops her character. We are not invited to think of her as unique but as commonplace, as the "common life" opposite of the Gothic heroine, even though Jane Austen cannot resist giving her a heroine's beauty. She is "a pretty girl" ten pages after her "thin awkward figure," "sallow skin without colour," "dark lank hair" and "strong features" (p. 13) have been used as satirical comment on the inevitable attractiveness of fictional heroines. But Catherine is, on the whole, developed by negatives: she cannot draw, cannot play the piano, has no opinions of her own and is naively literal even about matters one would have assumed her reading of fiction would have trained her to notice. Jane Austen also consistently describes Catherine in general terms. Comments on her reactions are frequently followed by generalizations about heroines or typical young ladies.

The final blow for Catherine's development as a unique and interesting woman is the parody scene in the bedroom at Northanger Abbey where several pages of mental process, usually an opportunity to create understanding of a character, are treated merely satirically. Jane Austen uses Catherine's fears to satirize the sensibility of the Gothic heroine. Even though this experience supposedly helps Catherine to learn that real fear is very different from the pleasurable horrors of Gothic fiction, it does nothing to create credibility in her sudden awakening from her fantasy world a few pages later. At a key point for establishing Catherine's validity as a maturing young woman, she has once again become merely the heroine.

There is never any danger that Catherine will develop attractive qualities which will become irreconcilable with her marriage to Henry Tilney. She remains the "female Quixote"[9] and never quite exists as Catherine Morland. As a female Quixote she must learn to reject a fictional view of the world and perceive reality. In *Northanger Abbey* these two worlds, the unreal or fantasy world and the real world, are clearly embodied in Catherine's two suitors: John Thorpe, brother of her new friend Isabella (who echoes his qualities), and Henry Tilney, a clergyman from Gloucestershire. The Catherine who meets them both soon after her arrival in Bath already has an unreal view of the world, whether because of her reading or her general naïveté is unimportant. She expects everyone to be either virtuous and straightforward or given to the sensational villainy that seems to be the result of living in abbeys.

John Thorpe is the antitype of the suitor as sinister villain. He is unscrupulous but his villainy is not of the dramatic kind. He boasts constantly about the abilities of his horses and the amount he can drink, and he has none of the charm of Jane Austen's later wrong suitors. He is completely self-obsessed, turning every conversation to his own activities. What is worse, he does not read novels and is ignorant of the fact that Mrs. Radcliffe wrote *The Mysteries of Udolpho.* John Thorpe is a liar, invents when it is expedient to do so, and disregards such simple contracts as Catherine's promise to take a walk with Elinor Tilney. John Thorpe's lying appears very often to be self-deception; it is undoubtedly his desire for Catherine's wealth which makes him invent it, boast of it to General Tilney and thus create the major disasters of the novel.

Catherine is in little danger of being attracted to John Thorpe; she early distrusts "his powers of giving universal pleasure" (p. 67). However, she does not immediately learn to reject what he represents in Jane Austen's scheme. His ability to deceive himself and to see things as he wishes resembles her own creation of a fantasy world. His inability to see the truth about others—he believes Catherine likes him—is similar to her own inability to perceive the true nature of such people as Isabella. His inexactness with language is parallel to the indiscriminate use of "nice" and "amazing" which Henry criticizes in her. It is no coincidence that in the novel John's first significant lie, which breaks Catherin's agreement with Elinor Tilney, is associated with a trip to the Gothic delights of Blaize Castle.

Henry Tilney is the Gothic hero reversed. He does, however, clearly embody the major virtues Jane Austen advocates in this novel. He is deliberately contrasted to John Thorpe: he likes novels and has read Mrs. Radcliffe with pleasure, is perceptive even about the value of muslin, is exact in his use of language, and concentrates on others rather than on himself. Most important, he understands the connection between honesty in conduct and language and the importance of contracts between members of a society. What Henry understands is that the society of laws in which they live and which keeps at bay the Gothic horrors which Catherine imagines, is founded on such open contracts. Correcting Catherine's suspicions of his mother's murder, he says "Does our education prepare us for such atrocities? Do our laws connive at them? Could they be perpetrated without being known, in a country like this, where social and literary intercourse is on such a footing; where every man is surrounded by a neighbourhood of voluntary spies, and where roads and newspapers lay everything open?" (pp. 197-98).

Walton Litz argues that Henry is undercut by Jane Austen, that he is shown to be what his sister accuses him of, "more nice than wise" (p. 108), and that his society of laws is exposed by his own reference to the actual Gordon riots of 1780 in an earlier scene.[10] But Henry's society of laws did survive the Gordon riots and Henry, although he sometimes sounds complacent, is well aware that villainy lies waiting outside the walls of his civilized world. Catherine may feel at the end that "in suspecting General Tilney of either murdering or shutting up his wife, she had scarcely sinned against his character or magnified his cruelty" (p. 247), but Henry has always known the true nature of his father. Nor is he totally devoted to the rational, knowing as well as Catherine that common sense cannot solve all problems, as he demonstrates by proposing to her in opposition to his father's wishes. He indeed has emotional intelligence.

Henry Tilney fully represents Jane Austen's views in *Northanger Abbey*. He is her echo from the beginning, adopting her tone as satirist and generalizing about Catherine just as she does. Of all Jane Austen's right suitors, except possibly George Knightley, Henry is most directly the heroine's mentor. He corrects her language, for example, and teaches her to appreciate landscapes. Even if he does not bring about the situation which results in Catherine's awakening, it is his rational reaction to her fantasies, we are asked to believe, which shocks her into the real world.

Certainly Catherine's maturity at the end of the novel

leaves something to be desired. Jane Austen asks us to believe that her heroine has gained perception; she may no longer be taken in by Isabella but she can still be deceived by the complexity of other characters. Henry knows a simple dinner will not be sufficient for his father, in spite of his protestations, but Catherine cannot understand "why he should say one thing so positively, and mean another all the while" (p. 211). However, she has at least learned the basic lessons that make future maturity possible. She has learned what Henry knew all along: that the real world is as dangerous, though differently so, as that of Gothic novels; that real people are mixed and complex; that one's protection in this society is openness of behavior, exactness of language, an awareness of and consideration for other people. Catherine has finally rejected what John Thorpe stands for and has become Henry —or is well on the road to it. But the reader is not distressed, mainly because it appears to be more interesting to be Henry than to be Catherine.

Although *Sense and Sensibility* alone among Jane Austen's novels appears to have two heroines, the Dashwood sisters, only Marianne goes through a process of maturing. Elinor is at the end what she is at the beginning, "the novel's standard of moral perfection."[11] She is the representative of "sense" in this novel only in the terms in which Jane Austen comes to define it, as a balance between emotion and understanding.

Elinor is equated with the right suitor Colonel Brandon and for much of the novel acts as his substitute as teacher for Marianne. This, indeed, is one of the problems with the novel because it allows Jane Austen to keep Colonel Brandon so far in the background that when Marianne marries him, the reader feels she is marrying a stranger. Marianne moves from identifying with Willoughby, the wrong suitor, to accepting the values of Brandon and Elinor.

Marianne Dashwood's problem is partly a problem of perception and in this she resembles other Jane Austen heroines; unlike Catherine Morland, who invents her world, Marianne is simply deceived by her own gullibility and by an appearance of truth. She has to learn to distinguish between what appears to be so from what really is. The value of social forms in relation to private feeling is the chief lesson that Marianne learns. Jane Austen's first criticism of the young Marianne is of her self-indulgence: her acute suffering (like Catherine Morland's delight in the Gothic horrors,) is shown to be at least partly enjoyable, and completely unmindful of the feelings of others; her sensitivity to nature, which some critics have found sympathetic, is revealed as largely literary. She is self-obsessed; her primary concern is her image of herself and, however one may judge the quality of her love for Willoughby later in the novel, at the point of his departure from Barton, it is surely little more than an adolescent infatuation.

Willoughby is the wrong suitor and as such is the embodiment of those qualities the heroine initially shares but eventually must abandon. His enthusiasm for Marianne's taste in literature is suspect from the beginning; the passages which describe it are lightly ironic. He is the charming rake from the novel of sensibility and has his counterpart in all Jane Austen's later novels. He has entered *Sense and Sensibility* in true romantic fashion, appearing just in time to rescue Marianne from a riding accident. He is attractive, reads with all the sensibility that Edward Ferrars lacks, but like Marianne, disregards the social forms and is inconsiderate of others.

These sins are shown to cover greater ones: not only does Willoughby's greed make him desert Marianne to marry an heiress, but as Colonel Brandon reveals, he has already seduced and deserted Brandon's ward Eliza. Greed and the tendency to reduce young girls are familiar traits in Jane Austen's wrong suitors and in Willoughby are ironically punished by his eventual realization that he does love Marianne. Willoughby's sins have been committed off stage— as sins always are in a Jane Austen novel—and it is possible that if he had not rejected so callously Marianne's desperate public displays of emotion in London, when he hid behind the very social proprieties he claimed to despise, that neither Marianne nor the reader would have been prepared to give him up. The weaknesses of charisma are hard to convey. But he does reject her and that rejection marks a turning point in Marianne's development.

It is the realization of Elinor's suffering for Edward, and more particularly of the intense nature of that suffering, which finally changes Marianne. She blames only herself. Marianne Dashwood, Jane Austen summarizes, "was born to discover the falsehood of her own opinions, and to counteract, by her conduct, her most favorite maxims."[12] A more sober Marianne is now one capable of some concern for others; she has not lost, as some critics claim, but gained from her change in values. The self-indulgence of adolescence is, surely, only attractive in a woman to those who prefer women to be children. Marianne has retained the best of herself; she is still the girl who "could never love by halves" (p. 379). If we feel, as Mudrick does,[13] that Marianne has been betrayed, it is, I suggest, because of a modern romantic preference for the open expression of emotion and a sympathy for the rebel that Jane Austen did not share.

But we do not find it difficult to accept her marriage to Colonel Brandon entirely without reason. There is nothing wrong with his character, of course; as the right suitor, he embodies all the virtues Marianne comes to adopt for herself. However, we see so little of him, and his long revelation of Willoughby's past and his own suffering is so undramatic that, although Jane Austen's view of him is clear, we have no chance to form an impression ourselves. Mudrick claims, with some justification, that his "abilities, interest, and pleasure are things that Elinor alone finds in the Colonel, that exist nowhere outside Elinor's mind."[14] The failure of execution with regard to the right suitor is particularly serious in a novel which uses so many fictional devices to create understanding for its sometimes undeserving heroine.

Although *Sense and Sensibility* is in some ways a richer novel than *Northanger Abbey,* Jane Austen's handling of the two suitors convention is not so successful. This is not, however, because of the greater complexity of the heroine but because of a failure to establish the validity of the right suitor. *Sense and Sensibility* does not illustrate a basic difficulty with the convention itself, but a flaw in Jane Austen's execution of it which might easily have been corrected without changing the thematic content of the novel.

The surface similarities between *Sense and Sensibility* and *Pride and Prejudice* are obvious. In both novels Jane Austen employs such fictional conventions as the villain whose charm obscures a past of greed and seduction and a hero who knows and later reveals this villainy. But, as Walton Litz says, in *Pride and Prejudice* the stale conventions become "a believeable part of the action and a natural vehicle for the novel's themes."[15] Wickham's elopement with Lydia is plausible and Darcy's revelation of his past weaknesses less stagey than Brandon's account of Willoughby's.

Few critics find any fault with the resolution of *Pride and Prejudice* but most attribute its success to the fact that both Elizabeth and Darcy change during the course of the novel and meet on some middle ground at its end. Elizabeth's emphasis on the individual's right to freedom from authority, on nature as the source of her judgments, is in contrast to Darcy's pride in his social place and acceptance of artificial restraints, this argument states; each ultimately reaches a balance between art and nature.[16] While this account is accurate enough as far as Elizabeth is concerned, it is a less than adequate description of Darcy. The Elizabeth described is the woman Jane Austen shows us in the novel; the Darcy is merely the man Elizabeth first sees.

Critics disagree about the success of Jane Austen's portrayal of Darcy's change, but no one seems to doubt that Darcy does change, that he moves from total concern with social form, with "art," to an acceptance of benevolence, of "Nature," just as surely as Elizabeth moves in the opposite direction. But, surely, this is not the case. Darcy always has "all the goodness";[17] he merely lacks the appearance of it. Once Elizabeth can see beyond appearances, she sees Darcy differently and so does the reader. Darcy has not changed, our view of him has. He is still what he always was: the correct balance between "art" and "nature," the right suitor, the moral norm of the novel.

The essential Mr. Darcy is suggested in his house, Pemberly, which Elizabeth so much admires on her visit to Derbyshire. It is a perfect balance between the artificial and the natural: "She had never seen a place for which nature had done more, or where natural beauty had been so little counteracted by an awkward taste" (p. 245). The master of the house is, according to the housekeeper, its equal; he has always been "the sweetest-tempered, most generous-hearted, boy in the world," "affable to the poor," "the best landlord, and the best master . . . Not like the wild young men now-a-days, who think of nothing but themselves" (p. 249). Even Elizabeth recognizes that this is significant praise: a blend of social duty and true feeling exercised with discretion. She begins to see that she has made an error in judging Mr. Darcy: Mr. Darcy has not changed. Far from being concerned merely with social forms, he is one of the few Jane Austen heroes described as feeling passion, as loving ardently. If he understands the necessity for some consideration of the social consequences before proposing to Elizabeth, his feeling are only "natural and just." If he hesitates before allying himself with Mrs. Bennet, Jane Austen does not criticize him for it; she objects to Mrs. Bennet's lack of restraint as much as he does. The Darcy whose discreet generosity rescues the Bennet family from the disgrace of Lydia's elopement with Wickham, is the same man who earlier went beyond his father's request in helping Wickham.

If we are deceived into thinking Darcy has changed as significantly as Elizabeth, it is because Jane Austen, far from making a mistake in execution, has pulled off a marvelous sleight of narrative skill. Elizabeth indeed talks of "such a change in a man of so much pride" (p. 266) and Darcy accuses himself of "pride and conceit," of being "selfish and overbearing," which he claims he "might still have been but for you, dearest, loveliest Elizabeth . . . . By you, I was properly humbled" (p. 369). This whole speech by Darcy suggests a much more fundamental change than has actually taken place and in some aspects it conflicts directly with the housekeeper's account of her master that we have been invited to accept as truth. Darcy may have become more sociable, more outgoing, but he has not abandoned pride which, after all, when under "good regulation," is hardly condemned in the novel. But Jane Austen wishes us to believe he has changed at this point because it is the idea of Elizabeth's influence upon him which most of all makes the correction of her "lively talents" and marriage to Darcy acceptable. Jane Austen has managed to use Darcy as a moral norm, as the traditional right suitor, without making the subjection of the heroine to his values seem a loss.

Elizabeth's acquisition of a balance between personal feeling and social restraint is not the only resemblance between her and Marianne Dashwood. Like Marianne, she forms and expresses her opinions too readily, though hers are more likely to be satirical than enthusiastic for she dearly loves a laugh; like Marianne also, her tendency to judge from appearances leads her to an initial attraction the wrong suitor, the charming rake George Wickham. (Her early dismissal of another wrong suitor, William Collins, can be seen as a rejection of an exaggerated stress on social form. Collins is too ludicrous a figure ever to attract Elizabeth, for whom Wickham's weaknesses are the only true temptation to make a wrong choice.) Wickham, guilty of the same sins as Willoughby, has "truth in his looks" (p. 86) and Elizabeth, as she later realizes, does not go beyond the surface.

In being universally popular, Wickham is set in opposition to Darcy, as in his boasting of his achievements and his tendency to judge from appearances. His favorite word of praise is "amiable": he wishes he could call Miss Darcy "amiable"; Mr. Bingley is "amiable and charming." Elizabeth in turn considers Wickham "her model of the amiable and pleasing" (p. 152). She is, of course, influenced initially by vanity, disliking Darcy because he has snubbed her, liking Wickham because he has flattered her with his attentions: "But vanity, not love, has been my folly" (p. 208). If Elizabeth does not suffer from her mistake to the same extent as Marianne does, it is partly because she does not have as strong a tendency to fall in love and partly because of luck. Wickham marries Miss King and reveals his true nature before Elizabeth has a chance to become deeply involved.

The most important aspect of Wickham's character, which Elizabeth initially shares and later rejects, is his disregard for social forms. The Elizabeth who argues with her Aunt Phillips in favor of marriages of feeling without fortune and despises her friend Charlotte for marrying William Collins without love, gradually comes to respect the social restrictions which inhibit the Wickhams of the world. When her sister as well as Darcy's has been seduced by Wickham, she is more than ready to accept Darcy's values. But this change began earlier, from the moment of receiving Darcy's letter of explanation, and can be seen in her new attitude to her father. Content to be his favorite daughter, sharing his ironic delight in the follies of others, Elizabeth had "endeavoured to forget what she could not overlook" (p. 236). But his failure to restrain the excesses of his wife's behavior has now touched her personally in Darcy's comments on her relations, and she realizes that the social proprieties protect everyone.

Elizabeth learns, as Marianne does, to respect the social forms, that first impressions are rarely just, and that the ideal is a balance between art and nature. But she is not harshly treated by Jane Austen; her intelligence, her warm feelings, and to some extent her wit are admirable qualities. Her maturing does not involve the sacrifice of any of them. Having adopted Darcy's values she can marry him, a marriage acceptable because we have been tricked into believing there has also been a fundamental change in Darcy. However, the two suitors convention works well here chiefly because the entire novel argues for the acceptance of some limitation on individuality and independence for both heroine and hero.

Mansfield Park is the least popular of Jane Austen's novels; perhaps not the least read—*Sense and Sensibility* probably has that distinction—but certainly the most actively disliked. Various reasons are offered for its unpopularity, but two of them are named most frequently: Jane Austen's abandoning of her usual ironic presentation and an unpleasant heroine, Fanny Price, whom Jane Austen asks us to admire and tries, perhaps against her true inclinations, to like herself. Mudrick claims that beneath the surface of Fanny Price's good qualities "we feel something persistently unpleasant—complacency and envy, perhaps; certainly an odd lackluster self-pity.[18] Kingsley Amis goes further than this and states that "Edmund and Fanny are both morally detestable and the endorsement of their feelings and behaviour by the author—

an endorsement only withdrawn on certain easily recognisable occasions—makes *Mansfield Park* an immoral book."[19].

Whether one is prepared to go as far as Amis or not, *Mansfield Park* is indeed a curiously flat book in which the virtuous characters, Edmund Bertram and Fanny Price, are less immediately attractive than two vicious ones, Mary Crawford and her brother, Henry, who becomes the wrong suitor. Mary Crawford has all the liveliness and wit of Elizabeth Bennet, and more sophistication, but these qualities are allied in her with a lack of moral standards acquired by living with a dissolute uncle. Jane Austen realized, one can assume, that the witty, ironic tone she had used so well in *Pride and Prejudice* and the earlier novels inevitably allied the reader with the witty characters of the novel. Henry Tilney's ironic vision, for example, is to a large extent Jane Austen's own. The use of irony against a witty character is something she does not attempt until *Emma*. In *Mansfield Park* she avoids placing the reader on Mary's side by making the tone on the whole literal and straightforward. There is irony in the novel but it is used almost exclusively against such minor characters as Mrs. Norris and Lady Bertram. Even then Mary's wit almost survives Jane Austen's condemnation and Fanny's virtue cannot compete with Mary's vivacity.

Mansfield Park is really an atypical Austen novel, one where the center of interest does not lie in the heroine but in the moral argument itself, an argument in which the heroine is little more than an everywoman. As such its treatment of the two suitors convention most closely resembles the novels I discuss in chapter two.

In *Emma*, perhaps the greatest of her novels, Jane Austen accepts two challenges: to create a wrong suitor who is not in any sensational sense a villain and to direct her irony against a witty and ironic heroine. Frank Churchill, wrong suitor, is much more successfully a villain of common life than is her first attempt at such a character, John Thorpe in *Northanger Abbey*. John's evils led to consequences that might well have resulted in serious physical danger for Catherine; Frank Churchill's are as significant, though not so overtly unattractive, but they never promise such disastrous results. He has only superficial resemblances to the wrong suitors of the other novels. He does not seduce young girls as Willoughby, Wickham, and Henry Crawford do; he merely flirts with Emma while secretly engaged to Jane Fairfax. He is not so obviously greedy as Walter Elliot and John Thorpe, though we have to assume that he keeps his engagement secret from Mrs. Churchill in order to protect his inheritance. He is more attractive than the other wrong suitors, "a very good-looking young man" with a face which "had a great deal of the spirit and the liveliness of his father's" and "a well bred ease of manner."[20]

In Frank Churchill, for the first time, Jane Austen shows what is wrong with such charm and social poise without allying them to sensational vices. Because he has always had everything his own way, it has been too easy to neglect social and family responsibilities. He does not even pay a visit to his father and new stepmother until long after their marriage and then only because his fianceé is living nearby. Emma does not feel she can "build upon his steadiness or constancy" (p. 265). In Frank Churchill, as in *Sense and Sensibility,* Jane Austen illustrates the dangers of not obeying the social forms and of failing to be what one seems. When Emma learns of Frank's secret engagement, she says "How could he tell what mischief he might be doing? How could he tell that he might not be making me in love with him? Very wrong, very wrong, indeed" (p. 396). Even when we are told his reason for flirting with Emma—he wished to disguise his true relationship with Jane—the explanation hardly seems adequate. There have been so many unnecessary insults to Jane, so much unnecessary conspiracy with Emma. He appears, indeed, to have enjoyed the tricks and games, to have enjoyed using people as his puppets.

Emma's faults are very similar to Frank's: she, too, enjoys using her wit and intelligence to maneuver others. In the creation of this heroine Jane Austen accepts the challenge of turning her wit against a witty character and in a series of dramatically ironic scenes traps a girl who thinks she understands and controls everything. Emma is a heroine whom Jane Austen herself claimed "no one but myself will much like"[21]

and very few have. Mudrick claims that "Emma has unpleasant qualities, which persist in operating and having effect."[22]
Mudrick is one of the commentators on Emma who find it
impossible to accept a tendency to manage other people's
affairs as a feminine quality. Like Edmund Wilson,[23] he seems
to believe that a desire to take the initiative rather than
follow, to act rather than be acted upon, makes Emma
mannish. Both critics accuse her of latent lesbian impulses.
Mudrick's dislike for this quality in Emma is made clear by
his using the terms "dominate" or "domination" five times in
two pages of his discussion of her character. But there is little
enough evidence for Emma's lesbian tendencies, something
which becomes abundantly clear if one compares this novel
with one written not long afterwards, Charlotte Brontë's
Shirley. Emma is no more capable of involvement with a
woman than with a man. That indeed is her problem: an
inability to admit her human interdependence.

Emma progresses towards a recognition of her own limitations and an acceptance of her need for other people. At least,
that is how Jane Austen wishes us to read the novel. Like
Catherine Morland, Emma has created her own world, and
has peopled it with the characters from her own life, but this
world is a fantasy because Emma does not perceive these
people accurately: Mr. Elton is not in love with Harriet but
with her; Harriet is not in love with Frank Churchill but with
George Knightley; Jane Fairfax is not secretly in love with Mr.
Dixon but with Frank Churchill. Emma's tendency to create a
fantasy world is suggested symbolically by her fondness for
charades, conundrums and other word games. This tendency
is echoed in many of the other characters in the novel: her
sister Isabella believes that everyone shares her obsessive
interest in her children; Mr. Woodhouse that Dr. Perry issues
health warnings which coincide with his own fears for
everyone's health.

Unlike the more static characters, however, Emma leaves
her fantasy world and, we are asked to believe, reaches the
reality represented by the right suitor, George Knightley. She
is a Mary Crawford who has a chance at the right moral
education. This education is provided by Mr. Knightley, who

is established early on as completely reliable and whose values Emma finally adopts for herself. Mr. Knightley is always what he seems, though it is worth remembering in our evaluation of the marriage that we feel less close to him than to Emma because we have never seen inside his mind. George Knightley is considerate of others, sending his carriage to take the Bates to the Coles' party, sending apples to cheer the Bates' winter, rescuing the snubbed Harriet at the ball, always arguing that such kindness is the duty of the more wealthy to the poor. After Emma's rudeness to Miss Bates at the Box Hill outing, he delivers a lecture on such responsibility.

Mr. Knightley's kindness to others is associated with his own responsibilities as a working landlord; the discussions between him and his brother clearly indicate this. His home, Donwell Abbey, like Mr. Darcy's Pemberley, is "just what it ought to be, and it looked what it was . . . the residence of a family of such true gentility" (p. 358). Mr. Knightley is, indeed, Jane Austen's representative in this novel of true gentility and as such has an accurate perception of the characters of others. He criticizes Emma's friendship with Harriet Smith, justly praises Robert Martin, sees the weaknesses in Frank Churchill, and knows that Mr. Elton is not the kind of man to make an unprofitable marriage. He shares Edmund Bertram's directness of manner and does "nothing mysteriously." He is more directly the teacher of the heroine than is any of the other right suitors except, perhaps, Henry Tilney. He always tells her the truth about herself: he "was one of the few people who could see faults in Emma Woodhouse, and the only one who ever told her of them" (p. 11). Mr. Knightley carefully creates a wife for himself in his own image. Emma, finally convinced by her realization of her love for Mr. Knightley that she has made a series of errors, attempts to correct her behavior to at least two people: Miss Bates and Jane Fairfax. She claims she has learned a lesson and thanks Mr. Knightley for it: "I was very often influenced rightly by you—oftener than I would own at the time. I am very sure you did me good" (p. 462).

What Jane Austen apparently wishes us to believe about

Emma's maturing is, then, clear enough: she has abandoned manipulation for human involvement, has abandoned the game-playing of Frank Churchill for the clear vision of George Knightley. The book presents the two suitors convention in its basic form, and the convention is acceptable because the sacrifices of the heroine are matched by a willingness to accept social obligation and restraint on the part of the hero.

However, In *Emma,* more basically perhaps than in any other Jane Austen novel, there is a problem with the final marriage. We have shared Emma's thoughts throughout. Wayne Booth claims this is a necessary device on Jane Austen's part to make an unpleasant heroine sympathetic: "By showing most of the story through Emma's eyes, the author insures that we shall travel with Emma rather than stand against her. . . . Seen from the outside Emma would be an unpleasant person."[24] Is this really so? Because Emma tells us she has achieved a basic reformation, we tend to believe it. But was Emma ever as bad as she finally comes to believe, even if judged by Jane Austen's own criteria for moral worth? Mr. Knightley eventually agrees that Emma's friendship with Harriet has done the younger girl good. Emma is not really totally lacking in judgment. "She was not much deceived as to her own skill, either as artist or musician" (p. 44); she has the social discretion not to argue with her brother-in-law; she tells her little niece to be "infinitely cleverer and not half so conceited" (p. 99) as she is; and she always trusts Mr. Knightley. When she is witty, don't we more often laugh with her than against her, as, for example, when she parodies Miss Bates? Aren't her vivacity and curiosity more attractive, and in the long run no more harmful, than Jane Fairfax's reserve? When Jane refuses to answer specific questions about the absent Frank Churchill, surely the reader as well as Emma finds it hard to forgive her? Moreover, Emma is not by any means generally unkind; the first impression we have of her is of her kindness to her father, of her concern for his welfare and of her tolerance of his eccentricities. Is Mrs. Weston really so far wrong when she says "With all dear Emma's little faults, she is an excellent creature. Where shall we see a better daughter, or a kinder sister, or a truer friend?" (p. 39).

Wayne Booth claims the marriage of Emma to Mr. Knightley is good because Emma needs correction. Edmund Wilson and Marvin Mudrick, of course, are sorry for Mr. Knightley: Wilson believes Emma will bring some new girl into the house and manipulate her life as she has Harriet's; Mudrick that Emma knows she will be able to assume her characteristic role after marriage and have everything her own way. But Emma has, after all, never had her own way with Mr. Knightley and he believes that marriage for a woman involves "submitting your own will and doing as you were bid" (p. 38).

If this marriage is unsatisfactory, it is so, I submit, because of Emma's strengths, not her weaknesses. The marriage involves abandoning some of these strengths along with her weaknesses and she has to accept more social restraint upon her personality than Elizabeth Bennet does in marrying Darcy. Jane Austen has suggested qualities in Emma,— initiative, an ability to organize, imagination,—which will find no outlet in this marriage. She looks forward to the same life, even to the same house. If the choice for Emma had been other than marriage or "woman's usual occupations of eye, and hand, and mind" (p. 85), she might, one suspects, have chosen differently. But this is very early in the nineteenth century and Emma does not quite escape the irony in which Jane Austen has bound her. The two suitors convention does not really fail here, but *Emma* illustrates the reasons it will fail in novels written later in the century.

According to my argument, *Persuasion* should be the Jane Austen novel in which the two suitors convention fails, in which we find the marriage of hero and heroine least satisfactory. This is the novel in which, for the first time, Jane Austen does not argue for some restraint of personal desire by social forms. There is no clearly defined, established society in which the heroine must find her place as the hero has before her. However, on the contrary, of all the marriages in Jane Austen's novels the marriage of Anne Elliot to Captain Wentworth at the end of *Persuasion* is probably the one readers delight in most. The reason is obvious enough: for the first time Jane Austen has written a love story, that is a novel where the suspense lies primarily in how two people, whose earlier engagement was broken, will find each other again. Moral values are not ignored, of course—this is, after all, a Jane Austen novel—but if the heroine changes her values in this novel, the change has taken place before the story begins. Anne Elliot learns nothing during the course of this novel except that Captain Wentworth is still in love with her.

The difference in tone in this novel is obvious at the end of chapter three where Jane Austen ends a chapter devoted entirely to the economics of renting Kellynch Hall by abruptly taking us inside Anne Elliot's mind where we are to remain for most of the rest of the novel: "Anne, who had been a most attentive listener to the whole, left the room, to seek the comfort of the cool air for her flushed cheeks; and as she walked along a favorite grove, said with a gentle sigh, 'a few months more, and *he*, perhaps, may be walking here.'"[25] The emotional intensity of this is allowed to stand without ironic undercutting and from then on our interest is centered in Anne's reconciliation with Wentworth. She is a heroine who vacillates between "joy, senseless joy" and "agitation, pain," the first Jane Austen heroine whose feelings are allowed to carry the reader with them. The reader even comes to accept small inconsistencies of characterization because of this as, for example, when Anne, who we have been told is the only one who can control her sister's children, has to be rescued from one of them by Captain Wentworth. We ignore the inconsistency because our attention is at that moment focused on Anne's emotion, which is communicated to us in a long, complex sentence that suggests her breathlessness.

Critics who claim that Anne Elliot is the moral norm of this novel are probably right.[26] At the beginning she has all the virtues that most other Jane Austen heroines only attain at the end of novels: she is kind, as her willingness to give up a social engagement to visit her sick friend, Mrs. Smith, indicates; is perceptive, for she makes no such mistakes as Elizabeth Bennet and Emma Woodhouse do in evaluating those around her; is constant, as her continued love for Wentworth shows; and is also capable, as her actions after Louisa Musgrove's accident reveal. If anyone learns in the course of this novel, it is probably the right suitor, Captain Wentworth. Wentworth, whose resentment at Anne's earlier breaking off of their engagement has led him to value firmness too highly, learns through Louisa's accident "to distinguish between the steadiness of principle and the obstinacy of self-will, between the darings of heedlessness and the resolution of a collected mind" (p. 242).

Despite this, Persuasion is, if read correctly, another instance of the successful use of the two suitors convention. This is the first and only novel by Jane Austen to be concerned primarily with metaphysical rather than moral matters. For whatever reason—perhaps the illness which killed her before this book could be revised—Jane Austen's vision of the world had changed. That is not to say that her values have changed, rather that she is more concerned with the framework in which they operate. The key to this is in the paragraph many critics use to argue, wrongly I think, that Anne Elliot does not regret having been persuaded by Lady Russell:

> Anne, at seven-and-twenty, thought very differently from what she had been made to think at nineteen. . . . She did not blame Lady Russell, she did not blame herself for having been guided by her, but she felt that were any young person in similar circumstances to apply to her for counsel, they would never receive any of such certain immediate wretchedness, such uncertain future good . . . she should yet have been a happier woman in maintaining the engagement, than she had been in the sacrifice of it; and this, she fully believed had the usual share, had even more than a usual share of all such solicitudes and suspense been theirs, without reference to the actual results of their case, which, as it happened, would have bestowed earlier prosperity than could be reasonably calculated on. (p. 29)

The world, Anne Elliot and Jane Austen now realize, is a world of chance, in which nothing can be counted upon for the future. It is a world in which "future good" is always "uncertain" but where things may "happen" for the good as often as they bring "solicitudes and suspense." Given such a world, Jane Austen argues for the validity of present feelings against the "over-anxious caution which seems ... to distrust Providence" (p. 30).

Jane Austen's concern with time is evidenced frequently in this novel: we see it in the changes wrought upon Anne's and Miss Hamilton's physical beauty, in William Elliot's reference to his change of belief, in the social changes which have forced Sir Walter Elliot to rent his house. Even Lady Russell describes herself now as "Being much too well aware of the uncertainty of all human events and calculations" (p. 159). Luck or coincidence brings about many of the events in the novel. This is always true in fiction, of course, but in *Persuasion* the author draws attention to the fact as, for example, when Anne comments that Louisa Musgrove's engagement to Captain Benwick is the direct result of the chance accident at Lyme. Anne's own reconciliation with Captain Wentworth is entirely fortuitous; it is mere chance that she stays behind when her family moves to Bath, and each of the events which follows has its element of luck.[27]

If we take the conflict in *Persuasion* to be between over-deliberate caution and a willingness to take risks, then the representatives of the two sides of the conflict are clearly the wrong suitor, William Walter Elliot, and the right suitor, Captain Wentworth. Wentworth belongs to the navy, the profession which has Jane Austen's strongest approval and which is constantly associated with taking risks. It is also the instrument of social change: Sir Walter objects to it as being a way for people of insignificant birth to rise socially. The navy is associated with informal, warm manners and with domestic happiness, as if the risks run make emotion valued the more. When Anne and Captain Wentworth visit the Harvilles at Lyme, she observes the warmth with which they treat him and the uncommon charm of their hospitality.

Social form is not praised in this novel. Propriety and formal manners are associated with excessive caution, with too great a degree of calculation, and ultimately with villainy. William Elliot, the wrong suitor, is finally unmasked as a true villain by Anne's old friend, Mrs. Smith, in a scene as bad as that of Colonel Brandon's revelation in *Sense and Sensibility*.

Even before that Anne has mistrusted him, although "his manners were so exactly what they ought to be" (p. 143). Anne distrusts him because he is overcautious, too deliberate, too cold, too unlike Captain Wentworth: "Mr. Elliot was rational, discreet, polished, but he was not open. There never was any burst of feeling, any warmth of indignation or delight, at the evil or good of others. . . . She felt that she could so much depend on the sincerity of those who sometimes looked or said a careless or a hasty thing, than on those whose presence of mind never varied, whose tongue never slipped" (p. 161).

Anne, in rejecting William Elliot and accepting Captain Wentworth, chooses love with all its risks over a cold, cautious safety, even if Jane Austen does tilt the scale a little by having the worst of Wentworth's risks over by the time the novel opens. What Anne has learned is that life is at best a risky business, however cautious we are, and that one of the few dependable things is love. By appealing for the first time to our emotions as well as to our judgment, in *Persuasion* Jane Austen has forced us to share her vision emotionally as well as intellectually. Love is triumphant.

In spite of the differences in Jane Austen's six major novels, the use of the two suitors convention in each one gives them a certain structural similarity: a heroine is presented with two sets of values, embodied in two men who are her suitors, and although her choice is often not in doubt, her actions always serve to expose the faults of one and the virtues of the other. The vices of the wrong suitor are similar in each novel: greed and selfishness, which are associated with violating society's code and frequently with charm. The virtues of the right suitor are kindness, duty to his neighbors, especially to those dependent upon him, and strong feeling balanced by a respect for the limitations imposed by established society. (Captain Wentworth may be an exception here.) The heroines are very different in personality—the liveliness of Elizabeth Bennet is in complete contrast to the reserved intensity of Anne Elliot—but as mature women they all share this balance of feeling with social responsibility and are in that sense echoes of the men they marry. Since the sacrifice of some aspects of self to the establishment is—except possibly in *Persuasion*—part of

Jane Austen's ethic for all her characters, we can accept it for her heroines. Only in *Emma,* where the heroine's modern strengths threaten to escape her author's vision, is there any hint of the trouble which the two suitors convention will cause fiction later in the century. The convention which Jane Austen established in the tradition of the British novel served her well.

Chapter Two

Aristocrat versus Commoner

ATHOUGH the most interesting part of a study of the convention of the two suitors is inevitably the discussion of its conflict with a more modern view of female maturity, it is necessary to realize that its successful use did not end with Jane Austen. Only the convention's continued and widespread use would account for its adoption by such novelists as Charlotte Brontë and George Eliot, for whose psychologically authentic presentations of developing women it presents serious problems.

As I explained in the introduction, the convention works well in novels where the development of the central female character is subordinated to thematic concerns or where she dies after choosing the wrong suitor and thus, obviously, never has to be seen as mature. In this chapter I am concerned with novels in which the two suitors convention is successful chiefly because the heroine functions as an everywoman and the main focus of the novel is upon ideas. None of these heroines has either the uniqueness or the credibility of an Elizabeth Bennet or an Emma Woodhouse. Such maturing as does take place in the heroine is one-dimensional in that the moral choice she exercises is not seen to modify her personality except on the most superficial level. If change takes place at all, it does not have that mark of psychological authenticity which above all holds the reader's interest in realistic novels.

Fanny Price, in Jane Austen's *Mansfield Park*, is typical of these heroines. She is dull not so much because she lacks vivacity and tends to preach but because she is static; she does not develop, even though the novel in its early chapters promises to concern itself with a girl's education. Fanny has learned all the basic virtues from her cousin Edmund, the right suitor, by the end of chapter four and Jane Austen has lost her usual means of creating tension in her plot through the mistakes her heroine makes on her journey towards maturity. Certainly Fanny's perception and morality are tested in *Mansfield Park* but her infallible rectitude is so firmly established that we do not for a moment imagine she will fall for the superficial attractions of Henry Crawford. As the novel progresses Jane Austen's moral vision may be clarified but no one is learning to accept it except the reader.

Since it does not lie in the heroine, the interest of these novels must lie in the moral conflict represented by the two suitors, in a battle between two views of life. I have chosen four from among the many novels where the convention works equally well because, although in some ways they are interestingly different, each involves basically the same conflict: one between aristocrat and commoner, a clash of classes in a variety of forms. I am using "aristocrat" in the widest sense to include both those suitors who are in fact titled and those whose social position is significantly superior to their rivals'. It is a theme which had an obvious appeal in a period when wealth, or the possibility of wealth, could challenge an aristocracy based on birth. It is not, of course, unique to novels with "everywoman" heroines and can also be found in other novels in this study: *Persuasion, The Egoist, Adam Bede,* and *Daniel Deronda,* for example.

In Mrs. Gaskell's *Mary Barton* (1848), a social problem novel about industrial conditions in Manchester between 1839 and 1842, the conflict is between rich and poor, between the son of a wealthy factory owner, Harry Carson, the false suitor, and a hardworking engineer, Jem Wilson. George Eliot's *Felix Holt* (1866), which I have chosen to discuss in this chapter because of its resemblance to *Mary Barton,* has Harold Transome in Harry Carson's role and Felix Holt in Jem Wilson's. Trollope's *Dr. Thorne* (1858) takes us back to the upper-class drawing rooms of Jane Austen's novels, a world now in decline. It contrasts another son of a self-made man, lazy, alcoholic Louis Scatcherd, whose father has been knighted for his achievements as a railway magnate, with Frank Gresham, a man of better birth but of less wealth owing to a failure in the family fortunes. Wilkie Collins's 1860 detective story, *The Woman in White*, pits honest drawing master Walter Hartright against evil Sir Percival Glyde. In each of the novels the aristocratic wrong suitor is seen as an upstart, in some way undeserving of his superior position, and the virtues of hard work are upheld in the right suitor.

The origins of *Mary Barton* lie, as commentators have pointed out,[1] in Mrs. Gaskell's own experiences in her husband's parish, particularly in the loss of her own child, which gave her increased sympathy for the lot of the Manchester poor. Although her solutions to England's industrial problems are hard to accept as viable today—like Dickens, she depends rather on awakening man's sense of his common humanity than on such political action as the Chartist movement—she undoubtedly achieved her aim of showing the poor that someone cared.

The social purpose of this novel is reflected in the generalized idealization of the workers and in the many didactic passages which make direct statements about their sufferings. The novel opens with a pastoral scene of a workers' outing in the fields near Manchester, where Mrs. Gaskell comments on "the acuteness and intelligence of countenance, which has often been noticed in a manufacturing population,"[2] and then focuses upon a supper where the Bartons entertain their co-workers the Wilsons. Their generosity to one another is stressed in their inclusion in the meal of old Alice Wilson, to whom even the Barton's meager cottage seems a palace. The sufferings of the workers—their poverty, the frequent industrial accidents, and the lack of health care— are emphasized also and are deliberately contrasted, in heavily didactic passages, with the plentiful comforts of the rich who can afford cold partridge for breakfast and cream in their coffee.

Mary, the heroine of the novel, is the daughter of a weaver,

John Barton, who was originally intended as its central figure and whose character is developed with a subtlety and complexity that far exceeds Mary's. Barton, whose sufferings and sympathy for those of others lead him to hatred and ultimately to murder, is the only character to transcend the documentary nature of the novel.[3] Mary clearly does not. Her story, her attraction to the son of the mill owner, Harry Carson, and her subsequent realization of her love for the honest workman, Jem Wilson, is merely an illustration of Mrs. Gaskell's theme; her choice simply particularizes the general truth of the fable: the necessity for unselfish human sympathy.

Since Mary's development is not central to this novel, the two suitors convention works well as a structural device. Apart from the unusual fact of her being working-class, she is a typical novel heroine of her period, and, as Margaret Ganz says, "lacks the depth and complexity to be a moving counterpart to her tragic father."[4] Mary is introduced in general terms: "Before my telling you so truly what folly Mary felt or thought, injures her without redemption in your opinion, think what are the silly fancies of sixteen years of age in every class, and under all circumstances" (p. 26). The folly referred to here is vanity—"Mary liked making an impression" (p. 30)—which has led her into a flirtation with Harry Carson, who, she thinks, can offer her a better life. "I was flattered by Mr. Carson, and pleased with his flattery" (p. 279), she explains later. But this weakness in Mary is insufficiently dramatized and therefore hard for us to take seriously, as is the danger of her following her Aunt Esther's footsteps into prostitution, a possible result, we are told, of such vanity.

Vanity and self-centeredness are qualities Mary initially shares with Harry Carson, the wrong suitor: "Her love for him was a bubble, blown out of vanity. . . . He had no doubt of the effect of his own personal charms in the long run; for he knew he was handsome, and believed himself fascinating" (pp. 101-102). He has no imagination for the sufferings of others, is prepared to seduce Mary, draws cartoons of the ragged strikers and, as representative of the employers, actually enjoys the excitement of the strike. As the master's son, he is the aristocrat of this novel, but his pretensions to class superiority are not very firmly based; his mother was herself a factory girl. The great class divisions which have arisen between employers and men, Mrs. Gaskell appears to be saying, cannot really be justified on the grounds of an understandable lack of comprehension of different social situations. The Carsons are not nobility, for whom there might be some excuse; they know firsthand the problems of the poor.

Harry Carson is deliberately contrasted with Jem: his wealth with Jem's poverty, his gaiety with Jem's seriousness, his expensive roses with the one flower Jem hopes Mary will ask for. Mary awakens to the difference between them early in the novel after rejecting Jem's proposal of marriage, an action which, somewhat unbelievably, brings her to suddenly realize her love for him: "She felt as if she almost hated Mr. Carson, who had decoyed her with his baubles. She now saw how vain, how nothing to her, would be all gaieties and pomps, all joys and pleasures, unless she might share them with Jem" (p. 114). She does not, however, see it soon enough to prevent Jem, who has been convinced by a well-meaning Aunt Esther of Mary's love for Carson, from challenging his rival on the street.

Harry is shot by Mary's father for political reasons and Jem falsely accused of his murder. Mary, who has turned her back on vanity but still has to prove herself worthy of the right suitor, does so by finding the one witness who can clear his name. Her own sufferings for Jem teach Mary to feel for the sufferings of others, a change of heart she illustrates for us by helping a hungry child. Her struggles on Jem's behalf, which dominate the second half of the novel, make Mary worthy of the love of the right suitor; she has acquired his moral virtues.

Jem Wilson has been characterized by those qualities which are the opposite of Harry Carson's. He is gentle rather than aggressive, as we see in his treatment of his young brothers, but capable of courageous action, as he demonstrates by rescuing his father from the fire at the mill. His hard work as an engineer gives him money which he unselfishly turns into a

lifetime income for his mother and Aunt Alice, an action
which fills Mary's heart with love "at this new proof of Jem's
goodness" (p. 126). His unselfishness even allows him to be
generous hearted about Mary's relationship with Harry
Carson: "If you mean fair and honourable by her, well and
good" (p. 152), he says to his rival. But the end of the novel
Mary has become Jem, unselfishly exerting herself for others.
Mrs. Gaskell even talks of her "worshipping" her future
husband (p. 306), but Mary's personality is not sufficiently
complex nor is the definition of female maturity in this novel
sufficiently modern for the reader to raise any serious
objections.

Apart from the interest created by the character of John
Barton, *Mary Barton* is a simple fable in which the conflict
between the two suitors is used successfully to illustrate the
importance of an unselfish understanding of others. On both
an industrial and a personal level Mrs. Gaskell believes these
qualities, which are embodied in her right suitor, to be the
solution to the problems of her society, "that a perfect
understanding, and complete confidence and love, might exist
between masters and men; that the truth might be recon-
gnised that the interest of one were the interests of all" (p.
331).

Felix Holt, set at the time of the first Reformed election in
the English Midlands borough of Treby, is in some ways
George Eliot's *Mary Barton* or *Shirley.* Its background is
industrial and social unrest—there is mention in the first few
pages of rick-burners, trades union and the Nottingham
riots—but its emphasis is on the viability of political solutions to these problems rather than on the sufferings of the
poor. George Eliot argues, as does Mrs. Gaskell in *Mary
Barton,* for the importance of the small, individual act of
compassion over sweeping reform or theoretical solutions.

The heroine of *Felix Holt* is Esther Lyon who believes
herself to be the daughter of the Reverend Lyon. The novel is
the story of her self-discovery, embodied and symbolized in a
very complicated version of the old inheritance and search for
identity plot. Esther's inheritance apparently belongs to
Harold Transome, the false suitor, who for self-seeking

reasons is running as a radical candidate in the upcoming election. The right suitor is Felix Holt, a watchmaker, who is a true radical though not a candidate since he distrusts the dishonesty of politics. The novel, then, sets up a choice between the aristocrat (here a false one since Harold is really the son of Matthew Jermyn, the Transome's family lawyer) and the commoner, the idealized craftsman Felix. Esther's development, we are asked to believe, is a gain in spiritual depth, a rejection of the values of material prosperity and social status for the recognition of the nonheroic small deed.

Felix Holt opens with the return to Treby of Mrs. Transome's son Harold, who had become a merchant and banker at Smyrna and is now a widower with a small son. His mother hardly knows him since he has written to her infrequently, a sign of the lack concern for others which characterizes his relationships generally. His attitude to women is that of a master to slaves; he hates English wives because "they want to give their opinion about everything."[5] It is significant that George Eliot chooses to suggest Harold Transome's arrogance through frequent comments on his attitude to women; it marks him far more clearly as the wrong suitor for Esther, who is struggling for self-identity, than would concentration on his other faults.

Nevertheless Harold Transome has many other faults. He places great emphasis on appearance and reputation and cares "keenly about making a good figure" (p. 111). His moral mediocrity is demonstrated most clearly in his decision to run as a radical candidate in the forthcoming election simply because he believes he has most chance of winning in that party, and in his willingness to associate, for political ends, with such men as the unscrupulous election agent, John Johnson. As always in a George Eliot novel, only after Harold Transome has suffered is there any indication that redemption is possible for him.

Esther Lyon, who originally shares Harold's shallowness and concern with appearance, is brought to vision and sympathy rather too quickly to be artistically convincing. Certainly, her vanities and weaknesses are not as subtly conveyed as those of Rosamund Vincy or Gwendolen Harleth and her maturing is not as successfully dramatized as Dorothea Brooke's. Indeed, there is altogether too little dramatizing of the early stages of Esther's growth, which is brought about almost entirely by lectures from Felix Holt. It is her ambition to be "a fine lady" that Felix Holt originally condemns in Esther; "a fine lady is a squirrel-headed thing, with small airs and small notions" (p. 153), he says, and refuses to admire her physical charms. She becomes aware that he sees her as trivial and selfish. Like Harold Transome, Esther is detached from the person she believes is her one remaining parent and is insensitive to his love for her. She finds his interests boring and objects to the smoky odor of his clothes. It takes Felix Holt to point out to her that her father's principles are worthier than her own.

Although she has a brief period of resenting Felix, Esther rapidly—indeed too rapidly—comes to accept him as her moral superior: "she felt herself in a new kind of subjection to him" (p. 213). Felix becomes her conscience, her inner check when she finds herself, as usual, making trivial and thoughtless remarks to other people. She begins to recognize her own weaknesses. She becomes more sensitive to her father. Her favorite heroes now seem merely decorative but she has hopes that Felix will change her life into something exalted, "into a sort of difficult blessedness, such as one may imagine in beings who are conscious of painfully growing into the possession of higher powers" (p. 327). Esther, thus, still desires a glorious life; she has merely changed her view of what is glorious.

The problem with the use of the two suitors convention in *Felix Holt* is not the fact of Esther's marriage to Felix. We can accept George Eliot's statement that Esther "was intensely of the feminine type . . . whose fullness of perfection must be in marriage" (p. 551). The difficulty is in the fact that she continues to idealize Felix long after her actions and judgment have shown her to have become much more than "a frightened child" with "a protector." George Eliot asks us to accept that maturity implies independence of judgment and clear-sightedness, but the mature Esther still sees Felix as "her hero" (p. 571) who is like "the return of morning" (p. 555). Harold

Transome's view of the relationship, in this instance, seems to be the perceptive one: "Esther's admiration for this eccentric young man was, he thought, a moral enthusiasm, a romantic fervour" (p. 577).

Felix is idealized not only by Esther but also by George Eliot. He is presented as Harold's opposite in his fight for honesty, in his attachment to his mother and to small children, and in his down-to-earth, rather humorless manner. His perception is shown by his ability to foresee what will happen to Esther; his words are frequently used by George Eliot for the purpose of foreshadowing. His lectures are invariably statements of George Eliot's views though they hardly endear him to the reader; we tend to feel with Esther that he should "found a sect" (p. 212).

If the two suitors convention does not create the problems for *Felix Holt* that it does for *Middlemarch*, it is because Esther has none of the intensity and moral fervor of Dorothea Brooke. We grant intellectual assent to the notion of her spiritual growth but have no emotional identification with it. Esther is never truly psychologically credible because her characterization lacks depth; many other heroines could take her place and we would never notice the difference. It is also hard not to see Felix Holt as her true superior. We are content, I think, that she should marry her teacher.

In *Dr. Thorne* Trollope takes us back to Jane Austen's world, the world of the drawing rooms of the landed gentry. Changes have taken place, however; money is becoming as important as birth and not even the De Courcys can any longer afford to ignore those who have made it in trade. The Greshams, the most important nonnoble family in the county, have had to mortgage some of their land to Sir Roger Scatcherd, an exstonemason, knighted for his activities with the railways, who now controls their lives economically. Frank Gresham, the young heir, must marry money to save the family fortunes, though he is in love with the poor niece of the doctor, Mary Thorne, the heroine of the novel.

Although he realistically observes the changes in his society, Trollope is basically conservative. David Cecil claims that Trollope "respected good birth."[6] He did not, however, admire good birth blindly; he has no respect for snobs, for the De Courcys, for instance, who are "prime examples of the fallacy of protecting the ancient lineage at the expense of the ancient virtues."[7] At the beginning of *Dr. Thorne*, he states his position clearly. The owners of the land, he claims, are the true aristocracy and the fittest to rule. Buying and selling, although necessary, "cannot be the noblest work of man."[8] Trollope respects the feudal ideal.

False aristocrats receive his strongest criticism. The Scatcherds have gained money and a title but have no possibilities of gaining the "ancient virtues" because of their birth. Lady Scatcherd with her working-class accent always finds her title an embarrassment. Trollope obviously has some respect for the industry of old Sir Roger but indicates the true unsuitability of such changes in social class in the second generation in Sir Roger's son, Louis, the wrong suitor. Although "there was nothing royal about Louis Philippe Scatcherd except his name" (p. 115), he is the upstart aristocrat of this novel through both his superior financial position and his inheritance of his father's title. Along with the title he has inherited all his father's worst qualities and none of his virtues; he is dissipated without being generous. Trollope snobbishly describes him as "acute, crafty, knowing, and up to every damnable dodge practised by men of the class with whom he lived" (p. 254). The most useful thing he does is die and leave his money to Mary Thorne.

Throughout *Dr. Thorne* there are deliberate contrasts drawn between Louis Scatcherd and the right suitor, Frank Gresham. Lady Scatcherd, as Frank's nurse, has even brought up both boys. When Louis is first introduced at his father's deathbed, Trollope explains that he is exactly Frank's age yet, because of his dissipated life, looks four years older. He is short and sickly, whereas Frank is a picture of health and strength. Indeed Louis's only function in this novel is as a foil for Frank.

Frank Gresham is the epitome of the English gentleman, with "a great love for his pure blood" (p. 315). But he is an English gentleman who is willing to adapt himself to a changing world and who is capable of carrying the "ancient

virtues" forward into this new world. With knightly constancy, he refuses to sacrifice his love for Mary Thorne to save the
estate, saying "I'll be a lawyer, or a doctor, or an engineer; I
don't care what" (p. 301). Trollope obviously admires his
independence while sharing something of the elder Gresham's
dismay at the prospect of a changing world: "Do something for
his living! And was the heir of Greshambury come to this" (p.
400). Trollope has the opportunity, as writer, to put this world
to rights, which he does by providing the Gresham estate with
the money Mary inherits from her uncle Roger Scatcherd.

How the marriage of Frank Gresham and Mary Thorne
comes about is the focus of *Dr. Thorne*. The two suitors
convention works here, in part, for the same reasons that it
works in *Persuasion*, because our attention is kept rather on
the problems of two young lovers than on the maturing of the
heroine. Mary Thorne, like Mary Barton, is not a girl whose
qualities seem to demand more fulfillment than she is likely to
find in a marriage to the right suitor. For all her "vehemence of
character" (p. 40) which causes her to defend an unjustly
accused servant girl, the pride she shows when rejected by
Frank's mother, and her good sense in not taking advantage of
Frank's first proposal, she is no Elizabeth Bennet. She is, as
Sadleir says, the typical Trollope heroine, willing to live
obscurely and dutifully, only demonstrating her womanly
strength at times of crisis.[9]

Mary Thorne, if she changes at all, moves towards acceptance of the world view the right suitor represents rather than
towards development of particular qualities of his character
which she already shares. She learns what the right suitor,
Frank Gresham, knows, that "love can only be paid in its own
coin: it knows of no other legal tender" (p. 474). But Trollope is
a realist and although he admires their willingness to put
feeling first, he does not put them to the test. He ends *Doctor
Thorne* by reestablishing the feudal world and restoring the
estate to those who have proved themselves possessors of the
"ancient virtues."

Wilkie Collins's *The Woman in White* (1860) is a mystery
story which skillfully employs the devices of later detective
novels—strategic switches in point of view, mistaken identity, imprisonment in isolated places and races against time—

to sustain suspense. It resembles *Mary Barton* and *Dr. Thorne* in its use of an "everywoman" heroine. Laura Fairlie, and in its thematic concern with the virtues of work and independence as opposed to the vices of arrogance and greed for unearned wealth. As in the other two novels, the virtues of hard work are embodied in the right suitor, a drawing master Walter Hartright, and their opposite in a pseudoaristocrat, Sir Percival Glyde.

There are two particularly interesting aspects to Collins's use of the two suitors convention in this novel. First, the heroine actually marries the wrong suitor before ending up with the right one, something which is made possible because of the existence of her double, a half sister named Anne Catherick. Second, both the suitors also have stand-ins who are more interesting than they are. The sinister qualities of Sir Percival Glyde are accentuated by the constant presence of a companion, the grotesque Count Fosco, who aids him in his attempt to gain Laura's money; Marian Halcombe, an independent woman and half sister to Laura on her mother's side, acts as a substitute for Walter Hartright for most of the novel. Although the two suitors convention works on the surface in the familiar way, the sympathetic figure of Marian and the count's admiration for her independence at least hint at an underlying criticism of woman's traditional role in marriage.

When the novel opens, the story is being narrated by Walter Hartright, the right suitor, whose name suggests all we really need to know about him. He is not a complex character but has all the gentlemanly virtues. His first action in the novel is to rescue a woman dressed in white, Anne Catherick, whom he meets wandering late at night in a London street. Marian Halcombe's later reaction to his account of this event echoes the reader's: "Your management of the affair might not have been prudent, but it showed the self-control, the delicacy, and the compassion of a man who was naturally a gentleman. It made me expect good things from you. . . ."[10] "Natural" goodness is one pole of Collins's value scheme; to be straightforward and without guile, to follow one's feelings, are seen as positive goods.

Hartright goes to Cumberland as drawing master for two young women, Laura Fairlie and Marian Halcombe, nieces of Philip Fairlie, a neurotic art collector whose lack of involvement with his nieces is in part responsible for the disasters which occur. As a drawing master, Walter Hartright represents the values of hard work and, implicitly, of the superiority of an honorable poverty and the simple life over wealth. In a discussion with Marian about her fantasies of marriage to Walter, Laura sees herself in a neat cheap gown, sitting at home waiting for him to return from work. Walter Hartright falls in love with Laura Fairlie but does not fight for this love although he knows she returns it. Only later, after testing himself in the wilds of Central America, does Walter return with enough strength and independence to put his world to rights. He claims that danger has taught his will to be strong, his heart to be resolute, and his mind to rely on itself, and he describes himself as "a changed man" (p. 369).

Laura Fairlie must be one of the most insipid heroines in all of English fiction. There is never a moment when we are really interested in her character; it is hard enough to sustain concern about her survival. She tells Walter when she first meets him that she will believe everything he says and this gullibility characterizes her completely. Her straightforwardness, which makes her tell Sir Percival of her love for another man, admirable though it may be, puts her even further in the evil aristocrat's power. She values simplicity and has a "natural intensity of aversion to the slightest personal display of her own wealth" (p. 47); she thus shares the "natural" goodness of the right suitor. Laura is idealized by both Marian and Walter and never transcends Walter's initial description of her as the woman who first gave form to his shadowy conception of beauty, "the visionary nursling" of his imagination.

Laura Fairlie, out of obedience to her dead father's wishes, fails to follow the dictates of her heart and agrees to marry the wrong suitor, Sir Percival Glyde. It is "the one fatal error of her life" (p. 175). Sir Percival Glyde is Walter's opposite. He has a superficial charm which makes Hartright call him at their first meeting "a gentleman, every inch of him" (p. 132) and even Marian concedes that he "is a very handsome man and a very agreeable man" (p. 170). But this charm is as little to be trusted as the charm of Jane Austen's wrong suitors. Unlike the straightforward Walter, Glyde is crafty, shrewd enough to obtain Laura's consent to their marriage while apparently giving her freedom to choose. He ultimately reveals his true nature, which is arrogant and cruel. Seemingly quite devoid of feeling, he tells Fosco he believes in nothing about Laura but her money and shows himself capable of her murder. Far from being the gentleman Walter thought him, he is finally exposed as a false aristocrat trying to hold on to a title which is not rightly his.

After Laura's marriage to Sir Percival, the story is continued by Marian Halcombe, who, being female and related to Laura, can reasonably be present where Walter cannot. Marian lives with the Glydes after their return from their honeymoon trip and thus observes the events which follow at first hand while Walter is in Central America. This was obviously a narrative convenience for Collins but does not explain why he found it necessary to make Marian take over Walter's role as right suitor as well as narrator. Marian Halcombe is described initially as the possessor of a "masculine look of the features" (p. 26), is proud of being talked to "as seriously and sensibly as if I were a man" (p. 200), and despises feminine characteristics as weakness: she tells Hartright "I don't think much of my own sex" (p. 27) and describes herself as "as inaccurate as women usually are" (p. 28); offering to work with Walter to support Laura, she says "What a woman's hands are fit for, . . . early and late, these hands of mine shall do" (p. 393). Marian's independence of spirit and courage are admired by Count Fosco who says to Glyde "Can you look at Miss Halcombe and not see that she has the foresight and resolution of a man? With that woman for my friend I would snap these fingers of mine at the world" (p. 293).

Far more than Walter Hartright, Marian Halcombe comes to represent the independence of the right suitor and, indeed, her feelings for Laura often seem more loverlike than sisterly. They are always described in the most intense terms: "His

Laura! I am as little able to realize the idea which those two words convey . . . as if writing of her marriage were like writing of her death" (p. 167), she writes ironically before the marriage to Glyde; after they have left, she is "blind with crying" (p. 176) and the thought of Laura's return keeps her "in a perpetual fever of excitement" (p. 178). Later, fearing danger for Laura, Marian "caught her by the hand as she passed me on her way to the table, and kissed her as if that night was to part us forever" (p. 260). I do not mean to suggest that there is any conscious sexuality here, only that Collins, in creating an independent woman, had no way to describe her except through attributes and behavior that are traditionally masculine. Like Charlotte Brontë in her creation of Shirley and George Gissing in his creation of Rhoda Nunn, Collins discovered his society lacked models and, indeed, language for female strength and initiative.

When the heroine makes the wrong choice of suitor, she usually pays for it with her life as Hardy's women do. Virginity is a prerequisite for marriage to the right suitor; no second chance is possible. There is an interesting illustration of this characteristic of the two suitors convention in The Woman in White. Laura Fairlie commits the great sin, her "fatal error," and marries the wrong suitor. But it is a marriage in name only; Glyde does not sleep with Laura because children would prevent his inheriting her money. He tells Fosco that Laura is not the least likely to leave children and Laura admits to Marian that "It is very hard for a woman to confess that the man to whom she has given her whole life is the man of all others who cares least for the gift" (p. 232). Since there is no real marriage to the wrong suitor, there is only a symbolic death. Anne Catherick dies in Laura's place and Laura, reborn, gets a second chance.

The Woman in White places a value upon independence even for a woman—Laura tells Marian to thank God for her poverty because it has made her her own mistress—but Collins avoids a conflict between this more modern view of female maturity and the two suitors convention by expressing it through Marian and keeping Laura dependent. Laura certainly gains some courage, enough to suggest her approximation of the virtues of the right suitor: she refuses to sign papers giving Percival her money; she expresses the wish to help earn her living and starts to paint. But true independence cannot be allowed her and Walter reveals that he was the only purchaser of her "poor, faint, valueless sketches" (p. 436).

The Woman in White does not seriously examine the problems of women, but it makes certain inferences. The independent woman remains unmarried; the married woman is either, like Laura, so idealized that we have no real interest in her or, like Madame Fosco, a caricature of female devotion. Only through Fosco's interesting final comment does Collins at all approach a direct statement of a more modern view of the woman's position in marriage:

> Where, in the history of the world, has a man of my order ever been found without a woman in the background self-immolated on the altar of his life? . . . I ask if a woman's marriage obligations in this country provide for her private opinion of her husband's principles? No! They charge her unreservedly to love, honour and obey him. That is exactly what my wife has done. . . . Your sympathy, Wives of England, for Madame Fosco! (P. 559)

But this view has not been sufficiently dominant in the novel and comes too late to prevent a successful use of the two suitors convention.

The novels discussed in this chapter are different from one another in many ways but they have a thematic and a structural similarity. All indicate a basic distrust of social position which is not founded on a true aristocracy of virtue: Harry Carson uses his position merely to flatter his own vanity; Harold Transome has no concern for other people; Louis Scatcherd has no sense of the responsibilities of money; Sir Percival Glyde is unfeeling and greedy. All the novels value work and see it as united to true feeling and compassion for others: the right suitors Jem Wilson, Felix Holt, Frank Gresham, and Walter Hartright share these qualities. In every instance the commoner defeats the aristocrat. Each novel makes successful use of the two suitors convention largely because the central female character is not complex and the novelist never engages our concern in her development. The appearance of the two suitors convention in these very different novels does something, I think, to suggest how widespread its use became in nineteenth-century fiction.

Chapter Three

Capital Punishment

CHOICE of the wrong suitor is usually punishable by death. Many nineteenth-century novels in which the heroine makes this error belong to a subgenre of Victorian fiction, "the social evil" novel. The error in these novels, is, of course, some unsanctioned sexual activity with the wrong suitor. Margaret Lane explains in her introduction to Mrs. Gaskell's *Ruth* (1853) that in Victorian fiction the seduced girl had three choices—emigration, prostitution, or death—and that, on the whole, the Victorian public preferred death.[1] Even Mrs. Gaskell, who is obviously sympathetic to her heroine's plight, kills Ruth off at the end.[2]

The heroines in some of these novels are simply unfortunate victims whose only defining characteristic is their slip from virtue, and, as types rather than individuals, they could as well have been discussed in the previous chapter. However, some of the erring women—Catherine Earnshaw,[3] Eustacia Vye, Tess Durbeyfield, Sue Bridehead—are much more interesting, at least potentially, than the Mary Bartons and Laura Fairlies. The convention of the two suitors works in these cases not because the heroine's character lacks interest but because her premature death prevents a concluding marriage and the inevitable equation of female maturity with the hero's virtues. We are invited to a funeral, not a wedding, and are thus never asked to accept the heroine's maturity as the conclusion of her experiences.

In the novels I shall discuss in this chapter, *Ruth, Wuthering Heights, Tess of the d'Urbervilles, The Return of the*

Native, and *Jude the Obscure,* the heroines all die, except in
Jude where Sue Bridehead ends in a living death. I would
suggest that their deaths do not only represent a concession to
Victorian morality. These novels can be read as psychological
allegory. In each of them, it seems to me, there is an implied
similarity between the heroine and her first suitor which
accounts, on a symbolic level, for the inevitability of his
return later in her life. This similarity is a fundamental
natural affinity which cannot be escaped; the first suitor's
return represents the reemergence of the heroine's true nature. Ruth, Catherine Earnshaw, and Hardy's heroines are
thus destroyed by their own natures, which return to haunt
them even after their establishment of new lives.

If we read the novels this way, it is necessary to abandon
the use of the terms "right" and "wrong" suitor because the
first suitor is not necessarily the wrong one. In fact, it
becomes very difficult to establish which is which. In
Wuthering Heights, for example, the first suitor, Heathcliff, is
the "right" one; in *Ruth,* the first suitor, Bellingham, is the
"wrong" one. The definition depends on the novelist's attitude
to the natural qualities the first suitor embodies. If he or she
sees them as dangerous and to be resisted, as Mrs. Gaskell
does, then the first suitor is the wrong suitor. If he or she sees
them as good simply because they are natural, as Emily
Brontë does, then the first suitor is the "right" suitor.

Mrs. Gaskell's *Ruth* is a moral tale, The heroine is a victim
and is treated sympathetically but is nevertheless responsible for her own errors. Sent at sixteen by her guardian to be an
apprentice to an authoritarian and unkind dressmaker, Mrs.
Mason, she has no real guidance. Life at Mrs. Mason's is hard
and Ruth has the darkest corner in the room. Mrs. Gaskell
calls her "innocent and snow-pure" (p. 43), tells us she knows
nothing about falling in love and introduces her to a charming,
wealthy young man called Bellingham who is also suffering
from the wrong sort of supervision; he has been spoiled by an
overindulgent mother. Mrs. Gaskell describes his attraction
to Ruth in terms that stress both her naivete and her natural
wildness. Bellingham likes her "simplicity," her "innocence,"

her "shyness," yet his impulse towards her is directed chiefly by the thought of taming her "wildness."

Ruth succumbs to Mr. Bellingham's seduction in part because of circumstances beyond her control but also because of the natural attraction she feels for him. She is not raped, struggles less strongly than Hardy's Tess and drifts into her first night with Bellingham much as Maggie Tulliver does into the fatal boat ride with Stephen Guest: "Her energy left her; she became stupid and languid, and incapable of spirited action" (p. 60). Mrs. Gaskell makes it clear that Ruth's prime motive is her infatuation with Bellingham: "strangest, dizziest, happiest of all, there was the consciousness of his love, who was all the world to her" (p. 58). Their vacation in Wales together is described as "true enjoyment" for Ruth, in terms which link her to what is natural, and her sin therefore becomes, if not excusable, understandable. Mr. Bellingham's sudden illness, his removal by his mother, and her own pregnancy, not guilt at wrong doing cause Ruth misery; guilt comes later when she understands more fully society's view of what she has done.

Ruth is rescued by a clergyman, Mr. Benson, and his sister, Faith, who pass her off in their community as a widow. Ruth educates herself in order to teach her son, Leonard, who is to be seen as the redeeming force in his mother's life. To support Leonord Ruth becomes a governess to the children of Mr. Bradshaw, a rigid and narrow-minded man who represents the strictest Victorian conventions. In his house she meets Mr. Farquhar, the other suitor, whom she sees as "a man to be respected and perhaps liked" (p. 188). In spite of being on the verge of an engagement to Jemima Bradshaw, Mr. Farquhar finds himself gradually becoming attracted to Ruth's calm dignity and beauty.

Significantly, it is at the point where a new relationship seems possible that the past returns. Mr Bellingham, who has changed his name to Mr. Donne, arrives as a guest of Mr. Bradshaw and, learning what has happened to Ruth, proposes to her. Ruth finds his voice "had yet its power to thrill" (p. 281) but she refuses him because her evaluation of people has been "raised and refined" (p. 281) and she no longer respects him. The past mistake cannot be put right by a later marriage.

Mr. Farquhar's true nature, not after all that of the ideal right suitor, is shown when Ruth's past history is revealed. He is relieved that he had acted cautiously and had not trapped himself in an engagement to a disgraced woman. Mr. Farquhar's actions, always prudent and often calculating, are set in opposition to the impulsiveness of Mr. Bellingham. Ruth may have taught herself a cool self-control but her natural impulses remain closer to Mr. Bellingham's than to Mr. Farquhar's.

There is some suggestion, it seems to me, that Mr. Bellingham's return not only reminds Ruth of her past sensuality but also forces her to recognize her present capacity to feel, to thrill to someone's voice even when she does not respect him. When Ruth, after she has survived nursing a fever ward full of patients during an epidemic, rushes to Bellingham's sick bed and dies as a result, she is not the victim of Mrs. Gaskell's concession to Victorian morality. The context is psychological rather than sociological. Ruth is punishing herself, not only for the past but for those qualities in her own nature which allowed the past to happen. In this sense Mr. Bellingham's words after her death are more significant than he knows: "I cannot tell you how I regret that she should have died in consequence of her love of me" (p. 449).

In would be hard to imagine two nineteenth-century novels more dissimilar in tone and values than *Ruth* and *Wuthering Heights* (1847). It is obvious that Mrs. Gaskell, in spite of her sympathy with Ruth Hilton and her desire to change society's attitude towards both the guilty woman and the innocent illegitimate child, is not on the side of the sexual passion which produces them. Emily Brontë, on the other hand, comes close to convincing us of the innate superiority of intense passion to all civilized moral codes. She is not, indeed, interested in morality; right and wrong, major concerns of most Victorian novels, have no place in *Wuthering Heights*. As David Cecil points out, "she sees human beings, not as they do in relation to other human beings, or to human civilization and societies and codes of conduct, but only in relation to the cosmic scheme of which they form a part." The emphasis of *Wuthering Heights,* particularly of the first part where

Catherine Earnshaw is the focal point and which is therefore my major concern here, is metaphysical.

In spite of the difference in their sympathies, Emily Brontë uses the two suitors convention in a way very similar to Mrs. Gaskell's. Catherine Earnshaw's choice is more clearly defined than Ruth's, but, like Ruth, she makes the wrong choice and dies for her error. Whereas Ruth dies for surrendering to her passion, Catherine dies for denying hers. She rejects the passionate part of her nature, represented by her childhood companion, Heathcliff, who has been degraded by her brother Hindley and who lacks education and social graces, and chooses the urbane, civilized Edgar Linton, who represents the calm world of Thrushcross Grange. She marries Edgar but, as in *Ruth,* the past returns in the form of the original suitor and Catherine dies as a result. The question of which is the right and which the wrong suitor is not seen in *Wuthering Heights* in terms of conventional morality; by all conventional standards Edgar is the better man. But he is not right for Catherine, whose deepest nature is identified with Heathcliff. Like *Ruth, Wuthering Heights* can be read as a psychological study.

The fact that the bond between Catherine and Heathcliff predates their adult consciousness of it is significant. Similarity of character in two children, whether or not it suggests a blood relationship as some critics have argued, certainly has the implications of a basic and natural likeness which it would not necessarily have in two adults more capable of moral choice. As children they are seen constantly against the rugged and stormy climate of the moors which is echoed in their own behavior. They are always in mischief, always exploding in violent expressions of feeling, always together. The impression of Heathcliff's "violent nature"[5] is heightened by Emily Brontë's frequent description of him in the imagery of wild nature: he is "an arid wilderness of furze and whinstone," "a fierce, pitiless, wolfish man," "an unreclaimed creature" (p. 87). Heathcliff recognizes their affinity, that she has "a heart as deep as I have" (p. 127), but the most direct expressions of it come from Catherine. In the scene where she explains her feelings to the housekeeper Nelly Dean before the marriage to Edgar, Catherine describes her love for Heathcliff as "the eternal rocks beneath," unchangeable, necessary: "Nelly, I *am* Heathcliff—he's always, always in my mind—not as a pleasure, any more than I am always a pleasure to myself—but, as my own being" (p. 70).

In spite of this bond, Catherine Earnshaw agrees to marry Edgar Linton who looks like a doll beside Heathcliff, "wanted spirit in general" (p. 56), and yet is handsome enough for Lockwood to understand her choice upon seeing his portrait. Both Nelly Dean and the reader do marvel at her decision, especially since her reasons for it seem less than adequate. Questioned by Nelly Dean, Catherine claims she is marrying Edgar because "he is handsome and pleasant to be with," "because he is young and cheerful," because he loves her and will make her "the greatest woman of the neighbourhood" (p. 66). It is difficult to tell whether vanity is Catherine's real motive: does she believe that marriage with Heathcliff would degrade her? Does she know that Heathcliff is her half brother and thus sexually taboo, as Q.D. Leavis suggests? Is she tempted by the civilized world of Thrushcross Grange? Does she hope, as she suggests, that she can help Heathcliff to rise by marrying Edgar? What is certain is that even as she makes the choice, she knows it to be wrong: "in whichever place the soul lives—in my soul, and in my heart, I'm convinced I'm wrong! . . . I've no more business to marry Edgar Linton than I have to be in heaven" (pp. 67-68), she tells Nelly Dean, giving as a reason for the statement the affinity of soul she has with Heathcliff. Catherine's error, then, is a spiritual one. She has denied her own nature in marrying Edgar and so in some way separated herself from the source which nourishes her, from Heathcliff and, transcending Heathcliff, from the vigorous aspects of the cosmos he represents.

Catherine is thus doomed once the marriage takes place, though it requires Heathcliff's return as an educated man and another parting from him, ordered by Edgar this time, to bring about the crisis which causes her death. Shut up in her room, pregnant with Edgar's child, she becomes deranged and recalls the miseries of childhood separations from Heathcliff. Heathcliff, of course, understands the cause of her illness: she is trapped in a narrow space, like "an oak in a flower-pot" (p. 131). Even Edgar has some inkling of Catherine's problem, wishing her up in the hills where "the air blows so sweetly, I feel that it would cure you" (p. 115). The violent scene of Heathcliff's reunion with Catherine in which he accuses her of betrayal makes the nature of her error clear. Heathcliff cries: "Why did you betray your own heart, Cathy? I have not one word of comfort—you deserve this. You have killed yourself" (p. 137). With what is almost her dying breath, Catherine admits her mistake: "If I have done wrong, I'm dying for it. It is enough!" (p. 138).

The choice of the wrong suitor is put right in *Wuthering Heights,* as in *Ruth,* through the next generation. After an abortive marriage to the sickly Linton Heathcliff, Cathy Linton, daughter of Catherine Earnshaw, who physically resembles her mother and bears her name, redeems her mother's error through a marriage to Hareton Earnshaw. The resemblance of Hareton, Catherine's nephew, to his aunt has haunted Heathcliff who, now in power at Wuthering Heights, out of revenge, brings up the boy in his own image. There is a new Catherine Earnshaw; like has finally returned to like, on a domestic rather than a mythological level—to use Dorothy Van Ghent's terms—and order is restored to the universe.

The two suitors convention, used to dramatize both psychological and metaphysical themes in *Wuthering Heights,* is admirably suited to Emily Brontë's purposes. Catherine does not mature during the course of the novel; she does not gradually acquire Heathcliff's—or for that matter Edgar's—virtues and surrender her personality to his. On the contrary, subordination of one's true nature is seen as destructive in this novel. Though the pattern of the novel works in the usual way with contrasts and similarities, the heroine's similarity to the hero is acceptable for two reasons: it is seen in terms of natural qualities rather than of moral virtues and, since it predates the beginning of the novel, it is not acquired at the cost of an earlier self the reader has come to know.

Wuthering Heights teaches us how to read Thomas Hardy. Emily Brontë would surely have agreed with his comment in the preface to *Tess of the D'Urbervilles* that a "novel is an impression not an argument."[6] This is not intended to suggest, as some critics have, that concern with Hardy's philosophical position is wasted effort since the philosophical passages are not integral to the works in which they appear and and do not in themselves form a consistent philosophical position.[7] Nor is it intended to deny that Emily Brontë perhaps deals with metaphysical questions on a deeper level than Hardy.[8] I mean rather that a comparison between Emily Brontë's use of the two suitors convention and Hardy's use of it in three of his most important novels, The Return of the Native (1878), Tess of the D'Urbervilles (1891), and Jude the Obscure (1896), reveals that they too reward reading as psychological studies of women.

Hardy's characters do not develop during the course of their experiences; they are essentially the same at the end of the novel as at the beginning.[9] For this reason the question of Eustacia's or Tess's or Sue's maturing is never relevant; they may change their opinions but not their characters. Indeed the desire for change, the yearning to be something other than what one is, which frequently expresses itself as a striving for outward change, dooms one in Hardy's fiction. Both men and women who suffer from "the ache of modernism," who are "touched by Promethean influences,"[10] are destroyed. Those, like Arabella in Jude the Obscure, who are content to adapt to things as they are survive. Hardy's disapproval of the person who struggles for a fuller humanity lessens as he moves towards the end of his career as a novelist until in Jude he reaches complete sympathy with him; however, as D.H. Lawrence puts it, "the aristocrat must die, all the way through: even Jude."[11]

When the central character is a woman, the pattern of a Hardy novel usually resembles that of the first part of Wuthering Heights: the heroine is involved in a relationship with a man whom she rejects and who returns to haunt and ultimately to destroy her later life with someone else. The reader and sometimes the heroine come to see that the man the woman rejected as the wrong suitor is actually the one whom she fundamentally resembles; his return symbolizes the resurgence of her true nature, which is inescapable. Hardy may not always admire this "true nature"—he certainly does not in the case of Sue Bridehead—but he nevertheless believes it to be unchangeable. He suggests this unavoidability of our place in the natural scheme by frequently showing us his characters against vast expanses of earth or sky. The initial bond between the heroine and the first suitor is often sexual, as in the case of Tess and Alec d'Urberville, and the resulting novel thus superficially resembles *Ruth;* the heroine is a girl attempting to overcome "a slip from virtue." This is not always the case; Sue Bridehead, for example, is attempting to escape a marriage she sees as a mistake.

In spite of a title which suggests that its major concern is with Clym Yeobright, *The Return of the Native* is really Eustacia Vye's book. Eustacia is one of Hardy's ambitious women, craving more than life seems to offer and seeing the opportunity for satisfying that craving only through men. Created almost twenty years before Sue Bridehead, Eustacia Vye has many modern impulses but none of the modern means of satisfying them. Nevertheless, the two suitors convention in *The Return of the Native* works well because Eustacia fails and we are never asked to accept the achievement of spiritual expansion through submission to another human being.

The natural environment against which the characters are seen in this novel—the bleak and rather depressing climate of Egdon Heath—is extremely important to *The Return of the Native.* Character is evaluated to a large extent by reaction to the heath: many of the folk characters—Christian Cantle, Humphrey the furze-cutter, Diggory Venn the reddleman—are inseparable from it; the main participants—Clym Yeobright, Damon Wildeve, Eustacia herself—have a more complex relation to it. Survival depends, as in many other Hardy novels, on adjusting oneself to what is given, to what is natural; destruction comes from attempting to reach beyond that. The heath is described as "a place perfectly accordant with man's nature—neither ghastly, hateful, nor ugly: neither commonplace, unmeaning, nor tame; but, like man, slighted and enduring";[12] the novel demonstrates the necessity of accepting this view of man's nature if one wishes to live.

Eustacia Vye is not a native of this land but an alien,

daughter of a Greek bandmaster and a woman from the fashionable seaside resort of Budmouth, now living with her grandfather in a cottage on Egdon Heath. She is first introduced in lonely isolation walking on the heath which she hates: "she felt like one banished; but here she was forced to abide" (p. 55). Eustacia's hatred of the heath will be her death; it is nevertheless seen as partly responsible for her dignity and for her melancholy.

In the early chapters of the novel Eustacia is described in terms that suggest superhuman stature: she has "Pagan eyes's; she looks like the Sphinx; she is "the raw material of a divinity" with "the passions and instincts which make a model goddess" (p. 53). It is this passionate intensity, her "flame-like" soul, which seems to characterize Eustacia best and which she has directed toward sexual relationships: "To be loved to madness—such was her great desire" (p. 56). To achieve "a blaze of love," she is prepared to challenge social convention and even to risk extinction. Her great tragedy is that she pays the price without gaining the reward.

When the novel opens, Eustacia has already become involved in a relationship with Damon Wildeve, a failed engineer. In spite of having the sensitivity of a Jude Fawley—he cannot "bear the sight of pain even in an insect" (p. 35)—Wildeve has caused suffering to Thomasin Yeobright by his continual vacillation between her and Eustacia. Like Eustacia, he hates the heath and offers to take her to America. He also shares Eustacia's "inflammability" (p. 50); it is not insignificant that the signal they use is the bonfire Eustacia lights on the heath. Eustacia does not recognize their similarities or, if she does, will not settle for them. Damon's love is too tame for her, she thinks, unworthy of the great passion of her soul. When Clym Yeobright, Thomasin's cousin, returns to the heath, Eustacia sees the possibility of a greater love and engineers a meeting with him: "Perhaps she would see a sufficient hero tonight" (p. 104).

At first Clym Yeobright appears to be that sufficient hero. A jeweler from Paris, he is associated in Eustacia's mind with the romantic world she needs. He has a superficial similarity to Eustacia; Humphrey observes to Sam "Both of them of one mind about niceties for certain, and learned in print, and always thinking about high doctrine—there couldn't be a better couple if they were made o' purpose" (pp. 85-86). Hardy introduces Clym in a way that recalls his introduction of Eustacia; he stresses his isolation and compares him to gods. Eustacia marries Clym but, in a reversal of appearances Hardy is to use again in the relationship between Jude and Sue, discovers that the apparent likeness masks a fundamental difference in nature. Clym loves the heath and "would rather live on these hills than anywhere else in the world" (p. 147). He has returned to be a schoolmaster and teach in his native land; he has rejected ambition and has come to view life as something to be accepted. So when his eyesight fails, Clym adjusts to life as a furze-cutter and becomes more closely one with his natural environment than even he had intended. Hardy describes him working on the heath as "a brown spot in the midst of an expanse of olive-green gorse, and nothing more" (p. 197). Eustacia, who had wanted a romantic hero, finds herself married to the heath she hates.

Inevitably Eustacia's natural longing for escape reasserts itself. Wildeve, who has unexpectedly inherited a fortune, is after all the man going to Paris and Eustacia agrees to see him again. When their secret meeting indirectly leads to Clym's mother's death and their discovery by Clym, Eustacia plans to run away with Wildeve although she knows he is not sufficient for her. Despairing of ever becoming "a splendid woman," Eustacia is drowned on the heath and Wildeve with her. The fundamental drive of Eustacia's nature, the longing for spiritual expansion which led her to the wrong choices, has finally destroyed her.

Tess of the d'Urbervilles is a novel of the same subgenre as *Ruth*. Like *Ruth*, it is the story of the seduction of a sixteen-year-old working girl by a rakish young man, the birth of an illegitimate child, and the girl's attempt to rise above her social disgrace. Like Ruth, Tess's past returns to destroy her present and she dies. Hardy is as sympathetic to his heroine as Mrs. Gaskell is to hers. The subtitle of the novel, "A Pure Woman Faithfully Presented," suggests this sympathy as does his comment in the preface to the fifth edition that "there was something more to be said in fiction than had been said about the shaded side of a well-known catastrophe."[13]

Many of Hardy's ways of creating sympathy for Tess Durbeyfield are similar to those employed by Mrs. Gaskell in defense of Ruth. Tess has been sent by her family to find employment with those she thinks are her rich d'Urberville relatives. She expects to work for Mrs. d'Urberville, but because of his mother's blindness is more dependent on the son, Alec, than she would otherwise have been. The seduction itself begins with Alec's rescue of Tess from some taunting work people and he uses his gift of a new horse to her father to increase her gratitude to him. Her ignorance and dependence certainly make it difficult not to see her as "more sinned against than sinning" (p. 205).

Nevertheless, her relationship with Alec d'Urberville does not stop after one night. She chooses to return to him, "temporarily blinded by his ardent manners, [she] had been stirred to confused surrender awhile" (p. 72). It is a purely physical relationship but not one, Hardy implies, that does not stir some sensual response in Tess. Indeed it is on the grounds of the naturalness of her act that Hardy makes his strongest defense of Tess. She is frequently described as part of her environment, as "a figure which is part of the landscape" (p. 248). As she walks alone in the woods after running away from Alec and returning home, she feels guilt but Hardy points out that "She had been made to break an accepted social law, but no law known to the environment in which she fancied herself such an anomaly" (p. 75).

As Steinberg says in his introduction to the novel, Hardy emphasizes her sensuousness and suggests "her capacity for deep sensual pleasure," in which respect "she has more in common with Alec than with Angel."[14] Alec's sensuality is apparent in all his actions, not only in his lust for Tess. He likes to ride downhill at full gallop, claiming "there's nothing like it for raising your spirits" (p. 43). Even after his temporary transformation into an evangelical preacher, the same sensuality is apparent in his face: "animalism had become fanaticism" (p. 271). In turning from Alec in dislike, Tess is, partially at least, turning from the sensuality of her own nature. If he is the "wrong man" for her, as Hardy frequently states in the early chapters of the novel, he is wrong because Tess, like Eustacia Vye, wants something more than the first suitor offers.

Tess has her "indoor fears" (p. 109), feelings which Hardy describes as those of the age, "the ache of modernism" (p. 110). The changing world of this novel, in which the railway runs and the beer has degenerated, has marked Tess with restlessness. After the death of her child and her attempt to establish a new life at Talbothays, it is this that makes her turn to Angel Clare, dimly recognizing perhaps, as Jude does later, the possibility of a better world in the intellectual pursuits Angel seems to represent. But like Clym Yeobright, Angel is a man who has abandoned a wider life for, in his case, a romanticized return to the land. He has rejected a life as a clergyman to learn farming.

In this as in everything else Angel Clare is in contrast to Alec d'Urberville, who is pretending to a higher social class. As several critics have pointed out, the two suitors are almost exact opposites.[15] Unlike Alec, Angel has a "self-controlling sense of duty" (p. 124) with women. He is lacking in sensuality: "not cold-natured, he was rather bright than hot" (p. 170); "his affection is less fire than radiance" (p. 213). He claims to love what is natural but is really drawn to the artificial; he enjoys the idea that Tess may actually be of good family while appearing to be a peasant girl. He believes that in choosing Tess he is choosing a "mate from unconstrained Nature, and not from the abodes of Art" (p. 154) but, as David Lodge points out, "he is constantly trying to dignify the homely pastoral in which he is involved . . . by talking to her about 'pastoral life in ancient Greece' and calling her by classical names."[16]

Tess models herself on Angel. She picks up "his vocabulary, his accent, and fragments of his knowledge, to a surprising extent" (p. 155). She adopts his likes and dislikes and has no wish opposed to his. Alec accuses her later, with some justice, of enslaving her mind to Angel's. Having superimposed upon her true nature a veneer of Angel's, she marries him. When she confesses the truth about her earlier relationship with Alec to

Angel, he responds in words whose irony he does not understand: "the woman I have been loving is not you" (p. 203). Alec is, indeed, as Angel says to Tess, "your husband in nature" (p. 215), and her awareness that in a physical sense Alec "alone was her husband" (p. 319) comes from something other than a guilty conscience.

Tess's return to Alec after Angel's departure marks the resurgence of the sensual in herself and it is this sensuality she tries to destroy by murdering him. Her death at Stonehenge is not just a sacrifice. She dies, in a place of pagan worship, for denying the sensuality of her own nature.

In some ways *Jude the Obscure* seems scarcely to belong in this discussion. It is Jude Fawley's novel more than it is Sue Bridehead's; one cannot argue, as with *The Return of the Native*, that the title belies the true focus of the book. Unlike the other heroines in this chapter, Sue does not die for her initial choice, although it seems legitimate to consider her return to the marriage with Richard Phillotson as a sort of death. Nevertheless, the pattern of *Jude the Obscure* is essentially the same as that of the other Hardy novels I have discussed. Once again the two suitors convention is successfully employed to illustrate a psychological truth about the central female character. Similarities and differences between characters are used more subtly than in *The Return of the Native* but the same reversal of appearances takes place. None of the apparent likenesses—that between Jude and Phillotson and that between Sue and Jude—proves as strong as the fundamental similarity between Sue and Phillotson. Although my discussion will concentrate on Sue Bridehead, it is important for an understanding of the structure of the novel to recognize that her experience with two men is mirrored in Jude's experience with two women.

In his 1912 postscript to the novel Hardy refers to a German reviewer who has written to him suggesting that Sue was the first portrait in fiction of a certain type of modern girl. The reviewer calls Sue "the woman of the feminist movement— the slight, pale 'bachelor' girl." He regrets that "the portrait of the newcomer had been left to be drawn by a man, and was not done by one of her own sex, who would never have allowed her to break down at the end."[17] In this final comment the German reviewer is probably wrong; one of her own sex would not necessarily have allowed Sue to succeed. Certainly no modern feminist can approve of Sue; she may be "dear, free Sue Bridehead" whom "Wifedom has not yet squashed up and digested . . . in its vast maw as an atom which has no further individuality" (p. 151), but it is not a true freedom nor a real independence. Sue Bridehead exploits the sexual relationship while denying its fundamental sexuality. She is what Jude calls her, a flirt. She herself admits that she needs the flattery of a man's love even if she does not care for him. She continually teases Jude in the same way as she has earlier exploited the Christminster undergraduate; she rehearses her wedding to Phillotson with Jude, denies him the right to love her and then encourages him to kiss her, and only agrees to sleep with him out of fear of his return to Arabella.

Unlike Eustacia Vye and Tess Durbeyfield, Sue lacks sensuality. Jude believes that she marries Phillotson without knowing what marriage means; certainly she regrets it. She compares sexual intercourse to the amputation of a limb—a strangely male image—and has such a physical aversion to Phillotson that she would rather sleep with spiders than with him. But things are not very different with Jude. She tells Jude, "My nature is not so passionate as yours" (p. 190) and he calls her "a refined creature, intended by Nature to be left intact" (p. 271), "the most ethereal, least sensual woman I ever knew to exist" (p. 273). For this reason, as D.H. Lawrence says, in marrying Phillotson she has married "the only man she could, in reality, marry."[18]

In one of the most insightful descriptions of the relationships in *Jude the Obscure*, Lawrence points out the basic similarity between Sue and Phillotson: "She made no mistake in marrying Phillotson. She acted according to the pure logic of her nature. Phillotson was a man who wanted no marriage whatsoever with the female. . . . For the senses, the body, did not exist in her; she existed as a consciousness.[19] Phillotson does indeed tell his friend Gillingham that he married Sue without understanding the demands of the daily communion of marriage and describes himself to Sue as "a bachelor by nature" (p. 185). When Sue leaves Phillotson he has already agreed to that sexless "mental communion" that she later seeks from Jude; it is, after all, only a chance error that he wanders into her room again one night and causes her to leap out of the window in revulsion. He would undoubtedly not have repeated the mistake if they had remained together.

It is hard to know exactly what Sue seeks from Jude beyond his devotion to her; perhaps the motivation to leave Phillotson is stronger than the motivation towards Jude. Sue has the habit of acting for negative rather than for positive reasons. Certainly she finds an intellectual bond with Jude and perhaps a spiritual one. Sue represents to Jude the best part of himself and he initially sees the relationship as a way of purifying himself from the sensuality that drew him to his first wife, Arabella: he tells Sue "All that's best and noblest in me loves you, and your freedom from everything that's gross has elevated me" (p. 210). It is not insignificant that he deliberately seeks out and cultivates a relationship with a cousin whose sharing of the family curse on marriage makes the barriers against their union doubly strong.

I do not mean to deny that Hardy sees much that is positive in their relationship. They are alike: Phillotson comments on "the extraordinary sympathy, the similarity between the pair" (p. 182); and Hardy himself talks of their mutual understanding which "made them almost the two parts of a single whole" (p. 231). But their basic natures are different. Jude cannot deny the sensuality in himself, cannot live in a sexless relationship with Sue who, although she bears his children, never accepts the sexuality. Her unwillingness to marry Jude suggests her reluctance to accept an obligation— albeit a legal one which Jude would never have used against her—to perform an act she dislikes.

When Phillotson reappears, Sue describes the pull of "conventions I don't believe in" (p. 260), but one wonders whether this is not really an expression of a desire to escape final commitment to Jude. The reappearance of Phillotson marks the reawakening of Sue's essential separateness, her asexuality. She returns to him, she claims, out of guilt, but she is really running back to a sexless relationship. Phillotson promises not to intrude upon her personal life. But this, of course, is no punishment for Sue and she has to punish herself for her true nature just as Tess and Eustacia do. Masochistically, she insists upon resuming the sexual relationship with Phillotson. Although Sue does not die, the novel ends with Arabella's speculations about her death.

The novels I have discussed in this chapter are similar in that they all employ the two suitors convention, to a greater or lesser extent, for a psychological purpose. The first suitor in each case represents an aspect of the heroine's basic nature which she attempts to deny but finds she cannot. The major implication of this adaptation of the convention is an interesting one: the nineteenth-century woman's true nature was irreconcilable with her social adaptation. If it could not be denied, sublimated in adjustment to the patriachal society, it was likely to destroy her. These heroines do not die for violating Victorian moral standards but for failing to be other than themselves.

Even without this variation, however, the convention would have worked well in these novels. It is successful primarily because the heroine dies for making a wrong choice[20] and, therefore, we are never asked to accept her maturity as synonymous with adoption of the values of a suitor. If *Tess of the D'Urbervilles,* for example, had ended with Tess's marriage to Angel Clare, whose views she had entirely adopted, the equation of female maturity with becoming the echo of a superior male would have been unavoidable. It is this implied equation which creates the structural problems in the novels I shall be discussing in subsequent chapters.

Chapter Four

A Question of Mastery:
The Novels of Charlotte Brontë

THE NOVELS I shall be discussing in the next three chapters return us, in one sense, to Jane Austen: they are all novels in which the maturing of a central female character provides the focus of interest. They all employ the convention of the two suitors, but in most of these novels, unlike Jane Austen's, this is a weakness and not a strength. The concept of female maturity has changed, has become more modern, and in various ways and to varying degrees comes into conflict with the convention.

This is not to say that the novels are necessarily less good than some of those in which the convention works well; it would be foolish to argue, for example, that George Eliot's *Middlemarch* is an inferior novel to Mrs. Gaskell's *Mary Barton*. The novels of Charlotte Brontë and George Eliot in particular are often richer for the very thing which creates conflict with the convention: the complexity of their view of women. But *Mary Barton* is structurally neater than *Middlemarch*, even if this neatness is achieved at the expense of complexity in the heroine's character. Both novels use the marriage of the heroine to the right suitor as a conclusion, but the marriage of Mary Barton to Jem Wilson is acceptable in a way that the marriage of Dorothea Brooke to Will Ladislaw is not. To *Middlemarch*, for all its strengths, the two suitors convention is a detriment and both George Eliot and Dorothea Brooke are its victims.

The three of Charlotte Brontë's four novels which employ

the two suitors convention are the subject of this chapter. *Jane Eyre* (1847), *Shirley* (1849) and *Villette* (1835) are all studies of developing women,[1] that is novels in which the heroine grows up during the action and is to be seen as mature at the close. The nature of this maturing is not the same as that which Jane Austen's heroines undergo; it is inner and spiritual rather than exclusively moral and is not necessarily marked by changes in social behavior. For example, to her acquaintances Lucy Snowe probably does not appear very different at the end of *Villette* from what she was at the beginning but the reader understands her to have experienced a fundamental spiritual growth. Emma, on the other hand, manifests her newfound maturity in such social action as paying duty visits to Miss Bates, and it is only through such changed behavior that her growth is apparent.

It is probably correct to attribute this difference, in part at least, to the influence of Romantic poetry upon Charlotte Brontë.[2] It is, however, important not to exaggerate or misinterpret this influence and to treat Charlotte Brontë's novels as self-indulgent wallowings in emotion in which feeling is valued for feeling's sake. David Cecil's comment that Charlotte Brontë's heroines "do not try to disentangle the chaos of their consciousness, they do not analyze their emotions and motives. . . . They only feel very strongly about everything"[3] is patently false. On the contrary, it is precisely a struggle between emotional self-indulgence and rational control that is a central theme of both *Jane Eyre* and *Villette*. Charlotte is far from Emily Brontë's position of valuing intensity of feeling for its own sake; this is perhaps the major distinction between the novels of the two sisters.

However Cecil is right when he states that all Charlotte Brontë's novels "are revelations of the same self."[4] He argues that since you cannot learn from observation about the inner life of anyone but yourself, all subjective novelists write about themselves. Therefore, he says, Charlotte Brontë's "characters are all the same person; and that is Charlotte Brontë."[5] The relationship between Charlotte Brontë's own life and her novels had long been recognized as significant. Letters, biographies, critical studies point out, among other facts, that Lowood in *Jane Eyre* is really the boarding school Charlotte and her sisters attended, that Shirley is a fictionalized portrait of her sister Emily, that both *The Professor* and *Villette* are based upon Charlotte's own experiences at a school in Brussels where she went first with Emily in 1842 and then alone in 1843 to study languages and prepare herself to be a teacher. The Brussels venture in which she came under the influence of and perhaps fell in love with M. Heger, a professor whom she describes as "my literature master—the only master I have ever had,"[6] is usually taken to be the formative experience of Charlotte's life. A good case can be made for this since both her first and last novels deal with it directly.

I suggest that all her novels can be seen as an attempt to come to terms with the significance of this experience, which was not merely a disappointment in love but apparently opened up in Charlotte a fundamental struggle between the implications of being master and those of being pupil. Numerous critics have pointed out that the master-pupil relationship characterizes the love affairs in all Charlotte Brontë's novels but they invariably conclude, I think incorrectly, that Charlotte really wished to be mastered. Walter Allen says "Fundamental to all her novels is the pupil-master relationship, which is her rationalization, based on her own limited experience of life outside Haworth, of one of the commonest sexual dreams of women: the desire to be mastered."[7]

Even Mary A. Ward in her introduction to *Shirley*—I say "even" out of the perhaps mistaken belief that a female critic can be expected to be more sensitive on this issue than a male—writes: "To Jane Eyre, Rochester is 'my master' from first to last; Louis Moore is the tutor and the tyrant even in love-making; Paul Emmanuel, for all his foibles and tempers that make him so welcome and so real, is still in relation to the woman he loves the captor, the teacher, the governor."[8] We can, of course, never be certain what was Charlotte's personal ideal and it is in a sense unimportant. The novels, however, make it clear that total dependence on another's will is no ideal for her heroines. Rochester is Jane Eyre's master at first but certainly not at last. We surely do not believe that the strong, independent Shirley of the first part of that novel is the same as the girl who accepts the control of Louis Moore at its close. Lucy Snowe finally takes from M. Paul not his mastery but the means to make herself independent of him.

Charlotte Brontë's heroines all struggle for their right to function as independent people and are therefore inevitably opposed to the nineteenth-century attitude toward women which lingers on even in modern critics who can seriously believe that any healthy individual wishes to be mastered. It is difficult to see how Charlotte, who wrote so much from her own experience, could have created a different sort of heroine. She had, after all, been independent and self-supporting most of her life and knew that this struggle meant self-regard and dignity as well as weariness. She was an artist and numerous letters testify to her recognition of the inevitable conflict in nineteenth-century society between being an artist and being a woman. Her desire to retain her pseudonym, Currer Bell, is essentially her desire not to be treated as "a woman who writes." She writes to George Lewes regreting that he insists on treating her work as the work of a woman; she responds to a review of *Jane Eyre* in the *Economist* with the words "To such critics I would say, 'To you I am neither man nor woman—I come before you as an author only. It is the sole standard by which you have a right to judge me—the sole ground on which I accept your judgement.'"[9]

Charlotte Brontë obviously valued sexual passion and knew what it meant. But she believed that passion inevitably meant loss of control, submission to the loved one, the master, and therefore a loss of independence. In all her novels mastery is associated with independence, control, and useful work; pupilage with dependence, passionate feeling, and submission.[10] Each of the novels from *Jane Eyre* on is a different attempt to reach a reconciliation between these two sets of values.

The Professor, written before *Jane Eyre* but not published until 1857, is Charlotte Brontë's first attempt to deal with the Brussels experience and also her first attempt at the master-pupil theme. Interestingly, it was originally given the title *The Master.* Since *The Professor* does not employ the two suitors convention, it is not central to my discussion, but it throws light on it by giving a very clear statement of Charlotte Brontë's ideal relationship.

The figure who represents Charlotte in this novel is a man, William Crimsworth, an English teacher who finds work in a school for young ladies in Brussels. There he meets and falls in love with a pupil, Frances Henri, to whom after various trials, he finally proposes marriage. It is the proposal scene which is of most interest. Frances accepts him, calling him "Master" twice in two sentences, and then, as they sit in front of the fire, gradually sets out the terms of their marriage. She wishes to retain her job as a teacher and is glad they have the same profession: "Thus we shall have both the same profession. I like that; and my efforts to get on will be as unrestrained as yours—will they not, Monsieur?"[11] Crimsworth replies insightfully "You are laying plans to be independent of me," which Frances grants is true. She wishes to be independent of him, but it is this very dependence that Crimsworth wants: "There is something flattering to man's strength, something consonant to his honorable pride, in the idea of becoming the providence of what he loves—feeding and clothing it, as God does the lilies of the field." Charlotte's use of the word "it" for "her" here is a masterly demonstration of her recognition of the similarity between the usual marriage relationship and a godlike ownership of an object.

Frances Henri listens to Crimsworth's description of what he earns and reacts in true feminist fashion: "Three thousand francs . . . while I get only twelve hundred!" But she still wishes to maintain her job after marriage, claiming she would be bored and therefore boring without it: "I have taken notice Monsieur, that people who are in each other's company for amusement, never really like each other so well, or esteem each other so highly, as those who work together, and perhaps suffer together." Crimsworth, surprisingly, recognizes the validity of this and agrees that hers "is the best way"; they marry and eventually open a school together. Charlotte's ideal is clear enough: it is a love between equals, sharing responsibility and working together but retaining their individuality.

The *Professor* does not resolve the master-pupil contest; this is partly because the game is played with false pieces. As an early reviewer in the *North British Review* states, Crimsworth is "a woman in disguise,—as indeed she proves to be,—for she is quite properly stripped of her male costume, and turned into 'Lucy Snowe' in *Villette*."[12] There are other problems with the novel. None of the characters has any real complexity and therefore no convincing confrontations of point of view take place. The scene I have described is not credible as an encounter between a man and a woman deciding their future. Everything is oversimplified; the two positions are merely stated, not dramatized; we have no sense that the problem is really engaged. *The Professor* is merely wish fulfillment. That Charlotte Brontë herself recognized this is obvious; she returns to the same situation in various forms in three subsequent novels.

Most critics, while noting the differences in tone, read *Jane Eyre* as if it were a novel by Jane Austen. For example, David Lodge points out that its strength lies in the fact that it is not a pure expression of Romanticism: "The instinctive, passionate, nonethical drive of Romanticism towards self-fulfilment at whatever cost, is held in check by an allegiance to the ethical precepts of the Christian code and an acknowledgement of the necessity of exercising reason in human affairs."[13] In other words, in spite of the fact the heroine's development is towards self-fulfillment rather than social conformity and in spite of the seriousness with which the gothic nature of the setting and many of the incidents are treated, the values advocated in *Jane Eyre* would not have been alien to Jane Austen. Charlotte Brontë's notion of maturity, like Jane Austen's, is described as a balance between passion and reason, as a reconciliation between "propensities and principles,"[14] even if she does stress, in this novel at least, the control of feeling rather than the learning of sympathy. I do not intend to suggest that this interpretation is false, but it is a distortion, for it overlooks a complexity in the character of Jane, and in Charlotte Brontë herself, which resists the reduction of the novel to such a simple formula.

Read in the usual way, Charlotte Brontë's use of the two

suitors convention also superficially resembles Jane Austen's. A heroine, Jane Eyre, plain and without a livelihood except that which she can provide for herself, has the choice of two men: Edward Rochester, the right suitor, who although it does not at first seem so, represents the virtues that Charlotte Brontë advocates, and St. John Rivers, the wrong suitor, whose values must be rejected. Jane matures during the course of the novel and eventually marries the right suitor.

The right suitor, Edward Rochester, is the owner of Thornfield Hall, a house to which he bears a strong physical resemblance, and the guardian of a child, Adele, for whom Jane Eyre has been hired as a governess. Rochester is undoubtedly, in many ways, the Romantic hero that critics have seen him as, a relative of those heroes of the Angrian world the Brontës created as children. He enters the novel by means of a horseback accident at dusk; he is "proud, sardonic, harsh," and unaccountably moody (p. 175), though hardly the monster Walter Allen calls him;[15] he is the jaded traveler who has sinned and whose soul, like Childe Harold's has surfeited. In Romantic fashion, he puts the highest value on individual judgement: "I shall judge for myself" (p. 146), he says to Mrs. Fairfax about Jane; and Jane calls him "an original, a vigorous, an expanded mind" (p. 306).

But he is more and other than this. This is not the Angrian world of moral chaos and Rochester is a reformed man. What is more, his reformation does not really take place at Jane's hands, though his redemption may. Rochester does not grow during the course of the novel; he is already reformed when Jane meets him, has already given up his mistresses and his wild life in Europe. Charlotte Brontë stresses Rochester's basic goodness: he tells Jane "Nature meant me to be, on the whole, a good man" (p.161); she believes him to be "naturally a man of better tendencies, higher principles, and purer tastes than such circumstances had developed" (p.176); the "wandering and sinful" man now describes himself as "rest-seeking and repentant" (p.264). In other words, the balance between passion and principle which Jane is to achieve at the end of the novel has already been learned by the right suitor before she meets him. We have Charlotte Brontë's own words for this in a letter to W.S. Williams: "Mr. Rochester has a thoughtful nature and a very feeling heart, he is neither selfish nor self-indulgent . . . he lives for a time as too many other men live, but being radically better than most men, he does not like that degraded life and is never happy in it. He is taught the severe lessons of experience."[16]

It is precisely these lessons of experience which Jane must undergo before she can become his wife. She already resembles him in basic character: he calls her "my equal . . . and my likeness" (p.308); she says they talk spirit to spirit, "just as if we both had passed through the grave, and we stood at God's feet, equal, as we are!" (p.307). Like him, she is "original," a word of high praise in the Romantic lexicon: her paintings are "original"; even St. John Rivers calls her "original."

Jane comes to Thornfield desiring "the busy world, towns, regions full of life" (p.129). It is this world, which Rochester has already seen, that he promises to show her: "all the ground I have wandered over shall be retrodden by you" (p.315). Ironically, in order to learn what he has already learned, Jane must leave him. Rejecting passion without principle, she refuses to be Rochester's mistress when, because of the continued existence of his mad wife, she cannot be married to him. She prefers being "free and honest" to being "a slave in a fool's paradise." What she still has to learn is that total control of passion, principle without emotion, is as ugly as its opposite.

This lesson is only really taught Jane, though, by the wrong suitor, her cousin, St. John Rivers, at whose house she arrives accidentally after leaving Thornfield. He and his sisters give her shelter and, after a time, although he loves someone else, he invites Jane to marry him and go with him as a missionary to India. St. John is Rochester's opposite, ice as opposed to fire, as all the imagery surrounding them suggests. Where Rochester is Romantic, St. John is Classic: he has "a Greek face, very pure in outline: quite a straight, classic nose; quite an Athenian mouth and chin" (p.421). Nature is no delight to him. "Reason, not feeling" is St. John's guide. Where Rochester values the individual will, St. John values obedience; his respect for forms makes him see Jane's going to India as his

assistant rather than his wife as an absurdity. Where Rochester is "rest-seeking," content with his life, St. John is a fanatic,
ambitious, desirous of change. Gradually Jane realizes that
life with St. John would be unendurable, that she could not
live "forced to keep the fire of my nature continually low"
(p.498)." If I were to marry you, you would kill me. You are
killing me now" (p. 504) she tells him.

Passion without principle may make one a slave, but
principle alone is harsher still. It is significant that a nonrational vision, Rochester's voice calling her name, is the cause
of Jane's return to Thornfield, of her discovery of the fire, Mrs.
Rochester's death, and Rochester's injuries. She is now
Edward Rochester's equal, having learned from experience
the need to balance passion and principle, and she marries
him. Read in this way, and many critics do read it this way,
Jane Eyre is a novel such as Jane Austen might have written
and the two suitors convention works well enough.

However, if this is the case, why did some early reviewers
consider the novel subversive? Kathleen Tillotson says these
reviewers heard the novel "as a voice from the dangerous
north and the dangerous class of oppressed or 'outlawed'
women; using it as a text on which to hang warnings about
female emancipation and a rebellious and un-Christian spirit
in society."[17] *Jane Eyre* is, indeed, "a feminist tract, an
argument for the social betterment of governesses and equal
rights for women,"[18] but not just in the sense that it has
usually been recognized as such. There are certainly overt
statements about the lack of work for women. There is the
often quoted passage about puddings and stockings: "Women
are supposed to be very calm generally: but women feel just as
men feel; they need exercise for their faculties . . . and it is
narrow-minded in their more privileged fellow-creatures to
say that they ought to confine themselves to making puddings
and knitting stockings, to playing on the piano and embroidering bags" (p.130). But the feminism of *Jane Eyre* is more
fundamental than this; it lies in what Jane herself comes to
represent and in the sympathy that Charlotte Brontë creates
for this. It is this sympathy which forces Charlotte Brontë into
a strange adaptation of the two suitors convention which, I
would suggest, does not quite solve the problem.

Charlotte Brontë employs the usual fictional techniques for creating sympathy for her heroine. Jane writes her story in the first person and proves herself a rational and analytic narrator whose comments on her own actions and on the characters of others it is easy enough to share. Her good sense allies us with her. What is more, Charlotte Brontë elicits our emotional response to the sufferings Jane must undergo. After Jane leaves Thornfield, her physical suffering when, starved and exhausted, she wanders looking for work is matched by her mental and emotional torment over the loss of Rochester. Our empathy with the adult Jane is, however, nothing to the sympathy Charlotte Brontë has earlier created for her as a mistreated orphan child. It is difficult, of course, for a reader not to respond to the sufferings of a child but what is important about the sympathy elicited for Jane is the particular quality of the suffering with which we are invited to sympathize.

Jane's suffering as a child in the house of her cruel aunt, Mrs. Reed, is presented in situations and images of imprisonment; what we are invited to share is her desire for liberty. Locked in the red-room after a fight with her cousin John, Jane sees that she is in jail and longs to "achieve escape from insupportable oppression." She sees this imprisonment as a punishment for uselessness, herself as "a useless thing," and associates it with being "mastered." Jane's first master is her cousin John, invariably referred to as the "young master" or "Master John," a tyrant and a bully, whom she is told she must obey because she is dependent. Opposition to the young master is described as the mutiny of a rebel slave. When Jane finally turns on Mrs. Reed in an outburst of anger, she experiences "the strangest sense of freedom, of triumph, I ever felt. It seemed as if an invisible bond had burst, and that I struggled out into unhoped-for liberty" (p.37). She soon learns this sense of freedom, born of unrestrained passion, is false, a form of madness.

True liberty, Jane's overwhelming desire throughout the novel, continues to be associated with opposition to "mastery," with independence, but with usefulness rather than with rebellion. Even though Lowood School provides her with some sort of livelihood as a teacher, Jane eventually comes to see it too as a "prison-ground"; she remembers that "the real world was wide" and wants to seek real knowledge of life amidst it perils" (p.98). The desire for experience is expressed by Jane as a longing for freedom: "for liberty I gasped; for liberty I uttered a prayer" (p .99).

This desire leads her to Thornfield and to a new position as governess, but she has little to do and still feels restless and unfulfilled. She is "weary of an existence all passive" (p. 137). The arrival of Rochester claims her interest, but he is a new "master," even if a good one, and she always refers to him as such. The word "master" reverberates throughout their conversations. Although increasingly attracted to him, Jane's willingness to obey "the master" is at odds with her fierce streak of independence long before the existence of Bertha Rochester is revealed. Even Rochester recognizes that Jane is unusual in her independence. He sees her as a bird in a cage: "a vivid, restless, resolute captive is there; were it but free, it would soar cloudhigh. You are still bent on going" (p. 165).

Before Rochester proposes, it is this sense of captivity which prompts Jane to make plans for departure: "I am no bird; and no net ensnares me; I am a free human being with an independent will; which I now exert to leave you" (p. 307).The basic problem of their relationship is avoided at this stage in the novel because the marriage cannot legally take place and Jane leaves in the name of morality, recognizing only the slavery of passion without the sanction of marriage vows. The issue avoided is the conflict between his mastery and her independence, regardless of the legal status of their relationship. When the marriage is originally planned, Jane wants to be financially independent of him: "I never can bear being dressed like a doll by Mr. Rochester, or sitting like a second Danae with the golden shower falling daily around me" (p. 326). (The sexual implications of this reference to Jove also perhaps suggest a reluctance to accept submission to Rochester's sexual mastery.) She is troubled by his "eastern allusions" and makes semiteasing comments about preaching "liberty to them that are enslaved—your harem inmates amongst the rest" (p. 327). She wishes to continue as Adele's governess and pay for her board out of that money. But Rochester's plans are different and his words are enough to strike fear into the heart of any independent woman: "'it is your time now, little tyrant, but it will be mine presently: and when once I have fairly seized you, to have and to hold, I'll just—figuratively speaking—attach you to a chain like this' (touching his watch-guard). 'Yes, bonny wee thing, I'll wear you in my bosom, lest my jewel I should tyne'" (p. 328). Figuratively speaking or not, Rochester obviously views marriage as the acquisition of a possession.

Jane's desire for liberty is strengthened by leaving Thornfield and the question of financial independence is eventually solved by the inheritance of her uncle's money. St. John Rivers is yet another master, both literally in becoming her teacher of languages and figuratively in offering to become her husband. "You shall be mine: I claim you—not for my pleasure, but for my Sovereign's service" (p. 491), he says to Jane. The thought of life with him once again creates images of imprisonment in Jane's mind, of "fetters," of an "iron shroud," and of a "rayless dungeon." This time there is no sexual attraction to blur the issue and she leaves him in a final act of self-assertion: "It was my time to assume ascendancy. My powers were in play, and in force. I told him to forbear question or remark; I desired him to leave me: I must, and would be alone. He obeyed at once. Where there is energy to command well enough, obedience never fails" (p. 514).

This is the true end of the story of Jane's struggle for self-fulfillment; she is now mature and independent. But it is not the end of the love story. The convention demands the heroine's marriage to the right suitor, as do sentimental readers, and Jane is returned to her master, as she continues to call him. Charlotte Brontë, however, appears to recognize that marriage of Jane to the old Rochester means submission to a master and is in conflict with her new found maturity. Financial independence, although stressed at their reunion, hardly solves the problem. So Charlotte Brontë maims him, depriving him of a hand and of sight, an act which several critics have seen as emasculation.[19] The relationship of equals which Charlotte Brontë asks us to accept in the final pages of the novel is apparently only possible once Rochester is no longer fully a man.

Even so, if we have understood Jane properly, we are, I think, left unsatisfied. Was all her new maturity, her understanding of the need to balance passion and principle, merely to make her worthy of Rochester? It has, after all, been learned from the experience we, as readers, have shared with her and we thus tend to grant it a credibility we cannot give to Rochester's wisdom. And her need for independence, her desire for rewarding activity, for new experience? Can these be satisfied in this marriage? Or has the vital, wilful, curious Jane, for all her protestations to the contrary, really been reduced to making puddings and embroidering bags?

In some ways, perhaps, *Shirley* is Charlotte Brontë's *Mary Barton;* certainly she felt so when she wrote to W.S. Williams, "In reading *Mary Barton* . . . I was a little dismayed to find myself in some measure anticipated both in subject and incident."[20] Like Mrs. Gaskell's novel, *Shirley* has a background of industrial unrest in the north of England; instead of Lancashire, the setting is Yorkshire in the latter days of the Napoleonic Wars when the closing of French markets to the Yorkshire woolen trade helped produce the Luddite Riots. Although this setting does affect the action of the novel, *Shirley* does not have industrial problems as its subject in the same way that *Mary Barton* does. Whereas Mrs. Gaskell's novel is weakened by her frequent generalization of the problems of workers, generalities in Charlotte Brontë's novel always give way to interest in the activities of particular individuals. There may be similarities in incident between *Mary Barton* and *Shirley,* but they do not really share a common subject.

The real problems with *Shirley* are structural. This is partly because of the difficulties in Charlotte's life when she was writing it. Each of the three volumes, was subject to what Winifred Gérin calls "the same ruinous break in continuity."[21] Charlotte Brontë began the novel elated by success of *Jane Eyre,* as the comic tone of the first chapter suggests, but as both her sisters Anne and Emily lay dying during its composition, the novel gradually became more somber and the two heroines, Caroline Helstone and Shirley Keeldar, took on the characteristics of Anne and Emily Brontë. Her duties as nurse and her suffering over their deaths must have made writing impossible for long periods. The structural problems cannot, though, be entirely blamed on these difficulties; they are next to inevitable given the characters she created and the convention within which she worked. In Shirley Keeldar Charlotte Brontë has created what Phyllis Bentley calls a "splendidly emancipated young woman" whose potentialities "there is really no action in the book sufficient to realize."[22] She might perhaps have added that they could hardly have been realized by any action in nineteenth-century England, at least none which the conventions of the novel would allow to be portrayed.

As if she realized the solutions of *Jane Eyre* were a romanticization, Charlotte Brontë begins *Shirley* with an address to her reader in which she promises them and perhaps herself to come to grips with reality: "Something real, cool, and solid, lies before you; something unromantic as Monday morning" (p. 1). In tune with this intention, she tackles her recurring subject, the question of mastery, head on; it is the novel's only major theme. She employs two heroines neither of whom can really be said to mature in the sense that Jane Eyre does; Caroline Helstone, however, moves in the direction of independence and Shirley Keeldar comes to accept dependence. They marry two brothers: Robert Moore, master of a mill, who is viewed by his workers as a tyrant, and Louis Moore, a tutor, who frequently refers to his own dependent position.

Shirley is a feminist statement; Charlotte Brontë investigates directly the question of whether or not an unmarried woman can find fulfillment. What kind of life could Jane Eyre have had if she had rejected St. John Rivers but not returned to Rochester? The life of single women is constantly referred to in *Shirley:* several pages are devoted to Miss Mann, whose sensoriousness is explained in terms of her life of self-denial, and others to Miss Ainley who has "tutored her thoughts to tend upwards to Heaven" (p. 400). Mrs. Pryor, who must function without a husband's support, reveals the indignities of working as a governess, but she does not think the married state much better. Talking of romance writers, she says to Caroline: "the false pictures they give of those subjects [love and marriage] cannot be too strongly condemned. They are not like reality: they show you only the green tempting surface of the marsh, and give not one faithful or truthful hint of the slough underneath" (pp. 388-89). The loveless marriages of Helstone and Yorke appear to justify this view.

Particular emphasis is laid on the powerlessness of women: "A lover masculine so disappointed can speak and urge explanation; a lover feminine can say nothing" (p. 106), Caroline says to herself after Robert's rejection. Rose Yorke expresses a longing for freedom similar to Jane Eyre's. Mr. Helstone's attitude to women is represented as typical of most men: "he could not abide sense in women: he liked to see them as silly, as light-headed, as vain, as open to ridicule as possible; because they were then in reality what he held them to be, and asked them to be,—inferior: toys to play with, to amuse a vacant hour and to be thrown away" (P. 118).

In the early chapters of the novel it seems clear that Caroline Helstone is to be its heroine. A niece of the rector, she is without financial independence and, although in love with her cousin, Robert Moore, has reason to believe that the romance will not lead to marriage. She is aware only of his apparent rejection, not of the business problems which are hindering his proposal. Some critics have speculated that Charlotte Brontë intended Caroline to remain single.[23] There is some evidence in the novel for this. Early on Caroline recognizes the greater freedom of a man's life and wishes nature had made her a boy instead of a girl. After Robert's apparent rejection, she struggles for a realistic view of her situation; she speculates on the uselessness of a woman's life without the duties of marriage and a family: "What am I to do to fill the interval of time which spreads between me and the grave?" (p. 179). Commenting on the "good works" offered by society as the sole activity of unmarried women, she remarks "Is there not a terrible hollowness, mockery, want, craving, in that existence which is given away to others, for want of something of its own to bestow it on?" (p. 180). She begs her uncle to allow her to earn her own living, even as a governess, but he has no understanding and tells her to run away and amuse herself. "What with?" Caroline says to herself, "My doll?" (p. 197).

Caroline certainly develops feminist views as the novel progresses; Charlotte Brontë even puts into her mouth the long and often quoted interior monologue at the end of the chapter entitled "Two Lives." For some four pages Caroline speculates on female education and the need for an occupation for single women: "Men of England! look to your poor girls, many of them fading around you, dropping off in consumption or decline; or, what is worse, degenerating to sour old maids,—envious, backbiting, wretched, because life is a desert to them" (p. 403). The words are eloquent and deeply felt but, I think, by Charlotte Brontë rather than by Caroline Helstone. It is hard to believe Caroline has changed; for all her words about female independence she is never seen as independent in character. After Robert Moore's guidance is removed from her, Shirley Keeldar's takes its place. When Caroline is first introduced, Charlotte Brontë announces: "So much for Caroline Helstone's appearance; as to her character or intellect, if she had any, they must speak for themselves in due time" (pp. 75-76). Somehow they never quite do; Caroline remains what Robert Martin calls her, "the epitome of the popular idea of the Victorian 'heroine': pretty, sweet, gentle, retiring, trembling at a frown, and with no particular gifts of intellect."[24] She cannot sustain the part Charlotte Brontë perhaps originally intended for her, though I suspect we were meant to believe in her move towards independence.

The suitor Caroline does not marry, and, of course, cannot since she is another woman, is Shirley Keeldar, the friend she finds after Robert's rejection. Once Shirley is introduced, she dominates the novel; it seems possible that Charlotte Brontë, recognizing that the question of mastery could never be resolved through Caroline, made a fresh start with Shirley. She is in many ways Caroline's opposite: possessed of an independent income and an accompanying independence of personality. She rejects the notion of marriage because "I could never be my own mistress more" (p. 219), an idea which she finds suffocating. She acts out her every whim and argues with Joe Scott for a woman's right to speak her mind. She fully understands the situation of women in her society. "If men could see us as we really are, they would be a little amazed" (p. 360), she says to Caroline, pointing out to her the artificiality of the heroines of male novelists. She has a vision of a "woman-Titan," as much "Jehovah's daughter, as Adam was his son" (p. 329).

Of course, Shirley's qualities are traditionally considered masculine ones and Charlotte Brontë falls into the trap that snares Wilkie Collins in his creation of the independent Marian Halcombe: she appears to be able to conceive of strength in a woman only in masculine terms. Shirley has a man's name and holds a man's position; she is fond of saying "I am an esquire: Shirley Keeldar, Esquire, ought to be my style and title" (p. 207). She even gets Mr. Helstone to call her "this captain of yeomanry, this young squire" (p. 209). She thinks of herself as a man and tends to consider her relationships with other women in this light: "If she had had the bliss to be really Shirley Keeldar, Esq., Lord of the Manor of Briarfield, there was not a single fair one . . . whom she would have felt disposed to request to become Mrs. Keeldar" (p. 211). She whistles like a man, conducts business like a man, runs freely around the countryside like a man, fancies herself a soldier, and even goes to defend Robert Moore's mill. Her fantasies are all of action: "I almost long for danger; for a faith—a land—or, at least, a lover to defend" (p. 310).

She is given the lover to defend in Caroline Helstone, whom she adopts much as Emma Woodhouse adopts Harriet Smith, although the homosexual undertones in the relationship between Shirley and Caroline are much more strongly marked. If we consider Shirley the heroine of this novel, then "the wrong suitor" is undoubtedly Caroline, though Shirley herself plays the role of wooer. It is not Caroline's qualities Shirley must reject but her own mastery, her control in this relationship. Unfortunately, although Charlotte Brontë may intend this intellectually, what she dramatizes is a character whose mastery is an essential part of her charm. When Shirley first meets Caroline, she presents her with flowers and looks at her "with something of the aspect of a grave but gallant little cavalier" (p. 206). She chooses to call her "Lina" because Robert Moore does and constantly imagines her as Robert must see her, putting herself in Robert's place: "Robert must think, as I think, that he is at this instant looking down on a fine face" (p. 238). She waits eagerly each day for Caroline's visit, resents Moore's interference in their friendship and even, teasingly, proposes a duel with him: "I feel disposed to call him out, if I could only get a trustworthy second" (p. 266). Caroline responds to this attention, which she has never received from Robert, and tells Shirley "I am supported and soothed when you—that is, *you only*—are near, Shirley" (p. 268). Shirley is always the leader, the protector. She watches Caroline like a lover, aware of her physical presence and compares their relationship to a marriage: "And are you so obedient to a mere caprice of mine? What a docile wife you would make to a stern husband" (p. 347).

Certainly married love is discussed by the two girls as something separate from their relationship and it is only very rarely considered in conflict with it, but whether she knew it or not, what Charlotte Brontë has described here is a love affair. Obviously, if Shirley is intended eventually to accept the mastery of a man, Caroline must be seen as the wrong suitor, but nevertheless Charlotte Brontë develops the relationship between the women in terms she usually reserves for a description of the heroine's bond with the man she is to marry. True to the two suitors convention, Caroline more and more comes to resemble Shirley and adopt her views, though she never becomes as strong or lively as Shirley. Like lovers in all Charlotte Brontë's novels, they have much in common: Shirley's height and shape are not unlike Miss Helstone's" (p. 205); they are both Yorkshire girls; Shirley finds "her own way of thinking and talking" understood by Caroline; their minds "often chimed very sweetly together" (p. 228). The word "suit," which Charlotte Brontë invariably uses to describe a good heterosexual relationship, is used here. Caroline thinks "we should suit: and what third person is there whose presence would not spoil our pleasure?" (p. 216);

"You and I will suit," responds Shirley, "I have never in my whole life been able to talk to a young lady as I have talked to you this morning. Kiss me—and goodby" (p. 222).

The implications of the mermaid fantasy Shirley describes to Caroline can be read as a comment on the true nature of at least Shirley's part in this relationship. Shirley imagines them both at sea: she is walking on deck, sees a mermaid, and calls Caroline up from the cabin. The mermaid has a human face, a face in the style of Caroline's. The mermaid behaves in siren fashion; it looks at them, "but not with your eyes," Shirley explains to Caroline; it has "a lure in its wily glance: it beckons" (p. 250). Being women, Shirley says, they can resist the mermaid where men could not. The mermaid dives down into the ocean again. What Shirley has acted out in fantasy appears to be her own rejection of a sexually alluring Caroline; the mermaid has Caroline's face but behaves more seductively. Shirley achieves the rejection by explaining to herself that women cannot attract other women. The basic pattern of the fantasy, though, suggests that the attraction exists, even if it is subconscious not only in Shirley but in her creator. The latent lesbianism of this relationship is obvious to a more sexually sophisticated twentieth-century audience. What is most interesting is that, ironically, it is the only relationship in the novel which convinces us of its warmth and humanity.

Most critics stress the fact that there are passages in which Shirley talks about a desire to be mastered.[25] Certainly there are such passages; she does say, for example, "Nothing ever charms me more than when I meet my superior—one who makes me sincerely feel that he is my superior" (pp. 221-22). She rejects Sir Philip Nunnely, who appears late in the novel to stand in for Caroline as a "real" wrong suitor, because "he would never command me. . . . And I know full well, any man who wishes to live in decent comfort with me as a husband must be able to control me" (p. 565). However, Shirley is hardly psychologically credible at these moments, and the scenes in which Charlotte Brontë tries to dramatize Shirley's acceptance of control by Louis Moore, the right suitor, are stiff and unconvincing.

Louis Moore is a representative of the combination of strength and dependence which we are asked to believe Shirley learns. He has been her tutor, but he only appears in the novel very close to its end, almost as if to provide a husband for the necessary concluding marriage. He is described as a backward and quiet and, as Martin says, has "an almost feminine gentleness."[26] He never comes to life and Charlotte Brontë is obviously uncomfortable with the relationship between Shirley and Louis. It is, therefore, incredibly awkward; for example, several pages are devoted to a composition Shirley wrote as his pupil.

Even if we can accept that Shirley is looking for her superior, it is quite impossible to believe Louis Moore is this man. Nor is the woman he imagines in his excessively long soliloquy the Shirley we have come to know in the novel. The last sections of the book are filled with images of Shirley as a captive animal, of Louis as her captor: "Lioness, she has found her captor. Mistress she may be of all around her—but her own mistress she is not" (p. 622). Can we believe that Shirley has simply capitulated? Is it Shirley who says "I am a woman: I know mine [my place]" (p. 635)? Who wants a husband to improve her? Who addresses her future husband as master, her "keeper" (P. 642), and makes no complaint when he says "You are younger, frailer, feebler, more ignorant than I" (p. 641)? Significantly, this relationship is described as her surrender rather than his victory. She has only found a master by reducing herself to the status of pupil; Caroline even quotes her as saying "Louis would never have learned to rule, if she had not ceased to govern: the incapacity of the sovereign had developed the powers of the premier" (p. 657).

By falling back on the two suitors convention, Charlotte Brontë has failed to provide a resolution for the real issues raised in *Shirley*. The question of mastery in relationships has not been solved. The novel ends neatly but falsely: Shirley Keeldar has been betrayed.

As critics always point out, with *Villette* we return to the material of *The Professor*. Once again Charlotte Brontë tackles her experiences in Brussels and her relationship with Monsieur Heger, only now from a perspective of six years and through a female protagonist. Margaret Lane says, "The *Professor* had been laid like a salve on a fresh wound, but now the scar would bear the artist's scrutiny; she was ready for *Villette*."[27] What critics point out less frequently is that *Villette* is as much related to Charlotte Brontë's other novels. As in *Jane Eyre* she takes a working heroine, but reverses the lesson she must learn: unlike Jane, who is naturally passionate and has to learn control, Lucy Snowe is initially controlled and learns to express feeling. In this novel Charlotte Brontë follows through on the ending she had probably intended for *Shirley:* she leaves her heroine unmarried. *Villette* is structured by means of the convention of the two suitors, but by avoiding the concluding marriage—the ambiguity about Monsieur Paul's death does not mask Charlotte Brontë's intention—she almost solves the problems involved in its use. That she does not quite succeed is perhaps less significant than the evidence she gives of her recognition of the problem.

Although *Villette* does not deal so directly with the question of mastery as *Shirley,* it places much more emphasis on the heroine's maturing. As in *Jane Eyre,* Charlotte Brontë uses a first person narrator but succeeds in taking us deeper into Lucy's mind and heart than she did into Jane's; Lucy Snowe's self-fulfillment happens on levels that Jane Austen never touched. The simplest way to describe Lucy Snowe's development is to say that she learns to open herself up to feeling;[28] it is as if Charlotte Brontë recognized that the imprisonment Jane Eyre felt could be self-imposed. Lucy is her own jailor. She does, however, come to accept more than that; acceptance of feeling is, inevitably, at least a partial rejection of reason, and to a large extent, Charlotte Brontë traces Lucy's development in terms of her awakening to the values of the nonrational, the world of the imagination. *Villette* is as much a Christian novel as *Jane Eyre,* but here Charlotte Brontë stresses the mysteries of God's will rather than Christian ethics.

Lucy's spiritual journey, like her actual one, can be read as a voyage from England to Belgium. England is made to represent a cool, rational, Protestant world where Lucy is constricted by herself; its spokesman is the wrong suitor,

Graham Bretton, who appears first as the son of Lucy's godmother and then as Dr. John at the girl's school where Lucy teaches in Villette. In Belgium, on the other hand, life is lived more intensely; it is a superstitious, Catholic world but one where Lucy gains true freedom. Its representative is the right suitor, Paul Emanuel, a professor at the school who is obviously based on Monsieur Heger. This scheme cannot be rigidly applied, of course; no one, for example, could be more calculating and rational than Madame Beck. Neither do I mean to suggest that Charlotte Brontë admires everything Belgian and disapproves of everything English, only that Lucy's gradual appreciation of the values of her new country are seen as a positive step in her maturation. Lucy does not become Catholic and Charlotte Brontë never abandons her own basic anti-Catholicism, but she does allow Lucy to learn respect for certain Catholic points of view. It is also true, perhaps, as Andrew Hook suggests, that Charlotte Brontë remains ambivalent about the value of the imagination and the implied loss of rational control.[29]

Granting these qualifications, however, the main direction of Lucy's development is clear enough. When we first meet Lucy at her godmother's house, she is a generalizer about life; although still young, she sees life as cruel and somber. Watching the child Paulina, she says "How will she bear the shocks and repulses, the humiliations and desolations, which books, and my own reason, tell me are prepared for all flesh?"[30] She finds nothing to change this view in her life as Miss Marchmont's companion or, at first, at Villette.

Lucy likes to represent herself as calm and lacking in imagination: she says she is "too prosaic to idealise" (p. 38); when Madame Beck asks her if she is too excitable to teach, she replies "I am no more excited than this stone" (p. 88); she has no desire to participate in the pleasures of going to a ball or opera, "only the calm desire to look on a new thing" (p. 125). She is in training for what she believes will be a life of suffering. She admits "she could feel" (p. 126), but believes all hopes for the future must be squashed. It is wrong, though, to think of Lucy as fundamentally cold even at the beginning of the novel; she has cultivated coldness out of fear of the intensity of painful feelings: "These struggles with the natural character, the strong natural bent of the heart, may seem futile and fruitless, but in the end they do good . . . they certainly make a difference in the general tenor of life, and enable it to be better regulated, more equable, quieter on the surface; and it is on the surface only the common gaze will fall. As to what lies below, leave that with God" (p. 210). For all Lucy's stress on the importance of appearance, she suggests here an awareness of tumultuous feelings below the surface.

Like all Charlotte Brontë's heroines, Lucy values independence, freedom, above everything else and she exercises self-control in the name of this independence. She is content if Madame Beck lets her work as she wishes. Loneliness is, of course, the inevitable result of the kind of liberty Lucy values; it is only later that she comes to realize that this liberty in isolation is really a form of imprisonment. The crushing emptiness of the school where Lucy, alone except for a mentally retarded pupil, spends the summer vacation, is a telling image of her spirit at this point.

Her strength, such as it is, can only be achieved at the expense of others; it is a form of negation. She controls her classroom by humiliating her pupils. Initially she adopts a superior and censorious attitude to everyone she meets in Villette: to the girls, to Madame Beck, to Ginevra Fanshawe. Anything which suggests pleasure or extreme emotion is associated in some way with Catholicism and has her strongest contempt. The emotionalism of Catholicism is in turn associated with the imagination, the nonrational; it is significant that Lucy cannot bear the violence of saint's legends read at the school in the evenings because they give her nighmares.

Charlotte Brontë skillfully reveals the weaknesses of Graham Bretton, the wrong suitor, even though this presents some problems. Lucy Snowe is the narrator and she is for some time in love with Bretton. Charlotte Brontë must, therefore, manage to have Lucy convey both the qualities that made him attractive to her and the underlying faults which, since they are her own initially, she cannot be too perceptive about. The result is the portrait of a man whose easy charm and spoiled upbringing have made him somewhat superficial;

he has never been required to look very far below his own surface or that of other people.

For all their differences in appearance and upbringing, the faults of Graham Bretton bear a close resemblance to Lucy's. His "straight Greek features" (p. 509) recall the coldness of St. John Rivers, which is also in Graham although in not nearly so prominent a fashion. He sits through the electrifying theatrical performance of Vashti unmoved, prompting Lucy to comment "his heart had no chord for enthusiasm" and to call him "Cool young Briton" (p. 308). The association of this quality in Graham with English Protestantism is frequently made. It manifests itself again in his rejection of the portrait of the voluptuous Cleopatra.

Beneath Graham's apparent selflessness, which is suggested in his work as a doctor, is a self-centeredness. Lucy says he has at times "a cruel vanity," a "self-love." He has "a consciousness of what he is" and "takes pleasure in homage, some recklessness in exciting, some vanity in receiving same" (p. 233). Although Lucy cannot be said to be vain in the same way, her initial inwardness and her insistence on isolation have the same quality of self-absorption.

Like Lucy, Bretton is unimaginative. She explains that the "sympathetic faculty was not prominent in him" (p. 223). If one expresses a need, he is ready to fulfill it, but he does not have much intuition in recognizing the needs of others. For this reason he is deluded by Ginevra Fanshawe, taking her for everything she appears to be on the surface. Graham Bretton is concerned with appearances much as Lucy is when she refuses to wear men's clothes when acting a male part in the school play. Lucy criticizes his attitude to Paulina very slightly since it is basically a good relationship and she may even be suspected of bias here. Nevertheless Charlotte Brontë does not undercut her observation that if Paulina had been of a lower social class Graham would not have seen her in the same way: "society must approve—the world must admire what he did, or he counted his measures false and futile" (p. 441).

It is, however, a dawning love for Graham Bretton that first begins to draw Lucy out of herself in the direction of expressed emotion. The summer spent alone at the school is the turning point for Lucy. For the first time she thinks of Ginevra Fanshawe with something other than contempt; she imagines the girl followed by "True Love" and sees her as a sort of heroine, though she calls this "a growing illusion," the result of overstretched nerves. It is during this period that, suffering from what today would be called a nervous breakdown, in desperation she visits a Catholic priest. He speaks a truth to her than she cannot at this point accept: "Protestantism is altogether too dry, cold, prosaic for you" (p. 190). Although she rejects this, Lucy recognizes the priest's kindness; for the first time she is able to see good in those who think differently from herself. She is beginning to extend her imagination in positive ways. The nun, who haunts the novel and is associated with the nonrational—significantly, Graham Bretton dislikes her—appears whenever Lucy has allowed herself to feel. For example, when she reads Graham's first letter in the garret, she sees the nun. Graham Bretton's letters allow Lucy for the first time to experience intense emotions. "Feeling and I turned Reason out of doors" (p. 301), she says.

By this time some basic changes have taken place in Lucy. She exchanges her gray dress for a pink one; she sees Vashti at the theater and is overwhelmed. She is ready for the relationship with Monsieur Paul and it is this relationship which finally brings her to a recognition of the value of feeling. Its climax comes in the festival scene when Lucy has been drugged by Madame Beck and, her rational faculties dampened, ventures out into the night: "Imagination was roused from her rest, and she came forth impetuous and venturous" (p. 539). During this night she overhears the Bretton party talking about their "steady little Lucy" who is always "so quietly pleased; so little moved" (p. 547) and is amused by the irony of this: "Little know they the rack of pain which had driven Lucy almost into fever, and brought her out, guideless and reckless, urged and drugged to the brink of frenzy" (p. 547). The surface Lucy has now been taken over by the real Lucy. Overhearing a false rumor about Monsieur Paul's forthcoming marriage to Justine Marie, she comments "I think I never felt jealousy till now" (p. 561).

In moving towards the values of feeling and the imagination, Lucy has gradually been approximating the qualities of the right suitor, Monsieur Paul, a Catholic professor at Madame Beck's school. In spite of their apparent differences, he tells her at the end of the novel that they are alike: "There is affinity between us. Do you see it, mademoiselle, when you look in the glass?" (p. 538). As always in Charlotte Brontë's novels, the heroine's faults may resemble those of the wrong suitor, but her fundamental nature is like that of the right suitor.

Monsieur Paul is superstitious; he believes in the nun and they see her together. He is associated with Vashti: "that gentleman had favored me with a glance which he seemed to have borrowed from Vashti, the actress" (p. 351); and he recognizes the voluptuousness of the painting of Cleopatra. He dislikes coldness; "his passions were strong, his aversions and attachments alike vivid" (p. 240); he is never reasonable. Unlike Graham Bretton, his superficial vanity masks a basically unmaterialistic nature; he values not the gift but the feeling that motivates it. Whereas Graham Bretton is described as "faithless," "the essence of Emanuel's nature is— constancy" (p. 472). He differs from Bretton most in the quality of his imaginative sympathy. To Lucy's surprise he guesses what sweet she would choose to eat; he guesses her mood accurately when she is depressed over leaving friends and when she is planning later to read Graham's letter alone. He knows her and we trust his assessment of her, even when, before we understand what he means, he says "You are one of those beings who must be *kept down*. I know you! I know you!" (p. 181).

As this quotation shows, Charlotte Brontë has once again been unable to avoid defining masculinity in terms of male domination of the female. Monsieur Paul's reference to "keeping Lucy down" occurs more than once; Lucy herself comments on it: "This idea of 'keeping down' never left M. Paul's head; the most habitual subjugation would, in my case, have failed to relieve him of it" (p. 433). But, although she remarks that she "did not trouble to be too submissive," one wonders whether Monsieur Paul would have accepted this independence in a wife. It is hard to overlook his stated view of women:

> A "woman of intellect" it appeared, was a sort of *lusus naturae*, a luckless accident, a thing for which there was neither place nor use in creation, wanted neither as wife nor worker. Beauty anticipated her in the first office. He believed in his soul that lovely, placid, and passive feminine mediocrity was the only pillow on which manly thought and sense could find rest for its aching temples; as to work, male mind alone could work to any good practical result. (P. 423)

Although Lucy's maturation is in the direction of awakening to feeling, and identification with another human being is therefore not in conflict with it, the problem of mastery has not been solved. There is no difficulty in accepting as evidence of Lucy's growth her increased valuation of the emotional intensity and colorful imagination of Monsieur Paul, but Charlotte Brontë has not found a reconciliation between independence and passion. To Lucy love is still bondage and though female independence and liberty are not stressed so strongly as in *Jane Eyre* or *Shirley*, Lucy Snowe values her liberty as much as do the earlier heroines. Running her own school is as important to her as it ever was to Frances Henri and it is not altogether the paradox she says it is that the three years of Monsieur Paul's absence were "the three happiest of my life."

It is clear that Charlotte Brontë recognized the dangers of the convention in which she was working, for she refuses the reader the usual romantic marriage of hero to heroine.[31] By leaving the question of Monsieur Paul's drowning at sea unanswered, she comes as close to an honest ending as in any of her novels. In terms of the qualities we have been invited to admire in Lucy Snowe and in terms of our understanding of the character of Monsieur Paul, this is also perhaps a happier ending for Lucy than a marriage would have been. However, it is not aesthetically satisfying; we are denied a sense of completion. The two suitors convention has provided the basic structure of the novel: the qualities of the wrong suitor have been rejected; those of the right suitor accepted. Omission of the concluding marriage for which we have been prepared has merely frustrated our expectations without solving the basic problem.

Charlotte Brontë never finds her way back to *The Professor*, where she had forced a reconciliation of mastery and pupilage, independence and marriage. Each of her subsequent novels attempts to reach a synthesis between a marriage of love and the heroine's fulfillment as an independent individual, but none succeeds. Jane Eyre's liberty is sacrificed on the altar of her passion for Rochester; Shirley's strength is negated to allow Louis Moore's weakness to triumph; Lucy Snowe retains her independence but is not allowed to marry Monsieur Paul. The unanswered question is to what extent these qualities are inherently irreconcilable and to what extent Charlotte Brontë has been trapped by the convention of the two suitors. The pattern of the convention demands a superior right suitor who, by embodying the virtues the heroine must learn, is inevitably her master; in each of Charlotte Brontë's novels this view of masculinity as mastery comes into conflict with the author's idea of female maturity. For Charlotte Brontë, independence and usefulness are necessary components of maturity whether in men or women. It is this modern notion of woman which is responsible for both the structural problems in her novels and three of the most interesting heroines in English fiction.

Chapter Five

A Wife Who Waddles:
The Novels of George Eliot

FOUR of George Eliot's novels that employ the two suitors convention[1] illustrate the uses of it that I have discussed in earlier chapters. *Adam Bede* (1859) is an example both of the aristocrat versus commoner theme and of the heroine who is punished for making the wrong choice. *The Mill on the Floss* (1860) is another "wrong choice" tragedy although the convention does not function in quite the same way as in Hardy's novels. In *Middlemarch* (1871-72) the convention causes structural problems similar to those in Charlotte Brontë's novels. In *Daniel Deronda* (1876), a flawed work in other respects, George Eliot's adaptation of the convention almost works.

One of the reasons we tend to agree with Virginia Woolf that George Eliot was one of the few English novelists who wrote for grown-up people is that she is concerned with problems that are clearly modern. Our own problems inevitably have an authenticity and a complexity hard to grant to those of earlier times which distance has simplified. George Eliot's world has the uncertainty of the twentieth century. No longer able to accept Christianity, having rejected her earlier evangelism, she struggled to discover a code of ethics to replace it. What she advocates in her novels is her own version of Feuerbach's religion of humanity,[2] replacing duty to God with duty to man. John Holloway quotes a letter written by George Eliot to the Honourable Mrs. Ponsonby in 1874: "My books have for their main bearing a conclusion . . .

that the idea of God, so far as it has been a high spiritual influence, is the ideal of a goodness entirely human."[3]

In a letter to Charles Bray that develops this idea further, she also claims that moral progress can be gauged by the extent to which we sympathize with individual suffering and individual joy.[4] It is this stress on the appeal to the individual situation over theoretical and general truths which characterizes her moral judgments in the novels. George Eliot comes very close to advocating situational ethics: "moral judgments," she says in *The Mill on the Floss*, "must remain false and hollow, unless they are checked and enlightened by a perpetual reference to the special circumstances that mark the individual lot."[5] Novel after novel makes the effect of one life upon another its central concern.

The function of art, as George Eliot sees it, is to extend our sympathies towards other human beings: "a picture of human life such as a great artist can give, surprises even the trivial and the selfish into that attention to what is apart from themselves, which may be called the raw material of moral sentiment."[6] At the beginning of book two of *Adam Bede*, she talks of the necessity for accepting people as they are, with all their flaws, and rejects the notion that a novelist should idealize. She argues for the portrayal of "real breathing men and women,"[7] "of commonplace things" (p. 172).

In George Eliot's world, compromise with the realities of life is always necessary; we never attain our ideals. She writes in *Adam Bede*: "And I believe there have been plenty of young heroes, of middle stature and feeble beards, who have felt quite sure they could never love anything more insignificant than a Diana, and yet have found themselves in middle life happily settled with a wife who waddles" (p. 171-72). The typical George Eliot character must always finally submit his individuality to his society, an act which Paris describes as the transformation of his "animal egotism" into "altruism."[8]

If this sounds like a description of Jane Austen's view, there are good reasons for it; George Eliot's values in many ways resemble Jane Austen's. However, whereas Jane Austen accepted her society and its traditions as givens, George Eliot does not. The difference between them is a question of response to what each saw as a human necessity. Both argue that compromise, the surrender of some part of one's individuality to society, is a requirement for survival, but George Eliot likes it less. Basil Willey's account of George Eliot in her later years reflects this attitude: "The keenness of her unsatisfied yearnings was tempered in her later years, but the clear-eyed endurance had strained her to excess, and the final calm seems in part to be that of exhaustion."[9] It is a description which might well have been applied to Dorothea Brooke at the end of *Middlemarch*.

This difference between the two novelists is the major reason why the two suitors convention causes problems for George Eliot that it did not for Jane Austen. It is true that her heroines can all be accurately described as egoists who are forced to submit their obsession with self to a more accurate perception of reality. Maturity for George Eliot undoubtedly lies in living without illusion, in doing without opium, but her attitude to this reduction of consciousness is ambiguous.

Barbara Hardy points out that George Eliot associates this necessary abnegation of self with the situation of women. Deprived of education and opportunity, Eliot's heroines build idealistic fantasies for which their lives provide no outlet, so that their final rejection of fantasy is hardly a matter of pure choice. The ambiguity of George Eliot's attitude to her heroines is, however, more fundamental than this. She does not merely sympathize with their condition; in many novels she betrays an admiration for their idealism which is usually linked to the idea of independent and altruistic action. While she conveys the egoism implicit in certain forms of idealism, she nevertheless appears to be emotionally drawn to idealists.

This can be explained in terms of George Eliot's own development, which is reflected in that of her heroines. At least three of her female characters—Maggie Tulliver, Dorothea Brooke and Romola—share important intellectual and temperamental characteristics with her.[10] George Eliot may be able to criticize those aspects of her own younger self which exist in her heroines, but some lingering regret over what they must give up remains. Compromise may be a necessity, but the ardent nature of her heroines, which is in conflict and must tempered, is nevertheless sympathetic. This sympathy, it seems to me, implies not only understanding but to some extent approval. They have what Henry James calls "an indefinable moral elevation."[11] Therefore, when a George Eliot heroine makes her compromise and marries the right suitor, who represents the new values, we are not altogether satisfied with the renunciation. Something we have been invited to admire has been sacrificed and we are asked to accept this as a good; the new values do not always seem to be a fair exchange.

Another reason that the two suitors convention frequently presents problems in George Eliot's fiction is that early in many of the novels the heroines seek satisfaction for their fantasies in the wrong suitor. Dorothea Brooke, Maggie Tulliver, Hetty Sorrel, and Gwendolen Harleth all do this. In the absence of opportunities for themselves, they seek a richer life through identification with the male's achievements. George Eliot suggests this is part of the problem. No man can be an ideal since all human beings have weaknesses, but the heroines initially lack the perception to realize this. Becoming aware of human fallibility is part of the maturing process.

However, because of the two suitors convention, the mature virtues are invested in the right suitor. The hero as mentor is a common figure in George Eliot's novels; Adam Bede, Philip Wakem, Will Ladislaw, and Daniel Deronda may have faults but they all function as examples and as teachers for the heroines. Barbara Hardy points out that "The hero is not only the male who is superior in education though with the same problems of feeling, but the lover with a particular understanding of the heroine's predicament, and often with an implausibly detached moral view of it."[12] The very figure, then, who represents the clear-sightedness and compromise the heroine must attain at the end of the novel, is idealized by the author. If the reader is invited to see him as an example, the heroine can hardly be expected to see him realistically. When George Eliot asks us to accept the maturity of her heroine, as in the cases of Dorothea Brooke, Esther Lyon and Gwendolen Harleth, she is showing us a woman repeating, in some sense, her earlier error.

Several critics claim that the endings of George Eliot's novels are unsatisfactory because of a conflict between her desire to portray the ongoingness of life and the basic concept of form.[13] All endings are necessarily artificial to her. Another reason for our disappointment in the endings, I would suggest, is the failure of the two suitors convention. Jerome Thale comes close to identifying this problem although he does not specifically mention the convention. Pointing out that we tend to prefer the unhappy or inconclusive endings to George Eliot's novels, he argues that when George Eliot grants her heroines apparent fulfillment, the ending is not satisfactory. The vocations of social service, small acts of kindness, or "marriage plus plain living and high thinking" are sketchily presented and made to carry more weight than they can bear. "Having seen the largeness of spirit of the characters and the magnitude of their errors, we expect that they should either attain a large fulfillment or else be left as failures,"[14] he says.

Adam Bede, George Eliot's first extended fiction, is set in feudal, rural England at the turn of the eighteenth century. It has the familiar plot of the naive peasant girl who is seduced by the young squire, impregnated, and then abandoned. In the terms I have been using in this study, it is a combination of the aristocrat versus commoner and the choice of the wrong suitor motifs. The aristocrat is Arthur Donnithorne, a young squire who gains his inheritance during the novel; the peasant girl is Hetty Sorrel, niece of a respectable family of tenant farmers, who is loved by the right suitor, Adam Bede, a carpenter. Adam Bede is also the right suitor to another girl— for this is a novel with two heroines—Dinah Morris, a Methodist evangelist, whose wrong suitor is Adam's brother Seth. Dinah finally abandons her evangelistic crusade and marries Adam.

George Eliot's journal reveals that the germ of *Adam Bede* was a story related to her by her Methodist aunt, who had visited in prison a condemned criminal, a girl accused of murdering her child, She had prayed all night with the girl who had eventually confessed her crime. The climax towards which George Eliot worked was this confrontation between the evangelist and the accused girl, between Dinah Morris and Hetty Sorrel, but the interest in the novel is really centered in the experiences of Hetty Sorrel.

Hetty is both pretty and vain: she has "a coquettish air" and devotes more attention to her appearance than to anything else. She constantly attempts to see herself in the mirror as she imagines others, particularly Arthur, will see her. Like all really vain women, she uses her beauty to gain power over others even if she has little or no feeling for them. She likes to feel Adam is "in her power, and would have been indignant if he had shown the least sign of slipping from the yoke of her coquettish tyranny" (p. 97).

George Eliot attributes Hetty's disasters in part to her lack of education and experience. She tells her reader to remember that Hetty is quite uneducated, a simple farmer's girl. But Hetty is not excused on these grounds; others almost as uneducated, among them Adam himself, are seen to be of stronger moral character. Hetty's lack is spiritual; she is simply "shallow-hearted," a flaw which crosses class lines. George Eliot states "we must learn to accomodate ourselves to the discovery that some of those cunningly fashioned instruments called human souls have only a very limited range of music" (p. 95) It is easier to accomodate oneself to the truth of this than to understand why, if George Eliot wished to write a tragedy, as many critics believe, she selected as her heroine a girl who had such a limitation. Hetty has very little understanding of what is happening to her. It is, indeed, misleading to call Hetty's story a tragedy at all.[15] The animal imagery associated with Hetty suggests that George Eliot is attempting to arouse sympathy for a victim, not tragic emotion for a noble figure. Hetty's inability to achieve full humanity is, on the other hand, an important aspect of that thematic concern with the distinction between the human and the merely natural which is treated more fully in Adam.

Hetty's ambition, her yearning for a better life, has none of the nobility we associate with George Eliot's later heroines. Her desire is to be a lady, to have wealth and status, and she sees Arthur Donnithorne as the means to that life. Nevertheless she shares with George Eliot's other heroines an egotistical tendency to fall in love with a false image of herself. Like them, she surrenders to the wrong suitor's attentions under the influence of "a pleasant narcotic effect . . . in a sort of dream" (p. 98).

Ironically, Arthur is a mirror image of the true Hetty, not of the one she dreams of being. He is charming, lives "a great deal in other people's opinions and feelings concerning himself" (p. 165) and shares Hetty's vanity. He has a vision of himself as the fine country gentleman, is a self-dramatizer and cannot really put anyone's suffering above his own. Even after learning of Hetty's imprisonment, he cannot help thinking that he too has been forced to give up his most cherished dreams. He is as weak as Hetty herself, unable to resist returning to the woods to meet her although he recognizes the potential danger in his actions. Arthur is not without conscience, but his conscience is shallow; he likes to be morally comfortable. He is capable of rationalizing almost anything and fails, until it is too late, to understand the harm he has done.

After Arthur leaves following his confrontation with Adam, Hetty becomes engaged to Adam, who has always loved her. As always in the novel of "wrong choice," the past reasserts itself. Hetty finds herself pregnant by Arthur and runs away to seek help from her cousin Dinah Morris. Unable to find Dinah, she has the child alone and in desperation, blaming the child for her problems, kills it. She is imprisoned for murder and remains in a state of shock until Dinah breaks through the shell of her defenses. Hetty confesses and feels remorse but never really matures. The two suitors convention works as far as the Hetty sections of the novel are concerned for the same reasons as it works in *Wuthering Heights* and in Hardy's novels, though it is not as subtly used in *Adam Bede*. We are never asked to accept Hetty as mature, merely as punished for her past.

Hetty's right suitor is Adam Bede who is deliberately contrasted with Arthur. Arthur himself contrasts his own "shilly-shally" character with Adam's firmness. Adam is the idealized common man;[6] as George Eliot says, "not an average man" (p. 204). When we see him first, he is in a natural setting, and he argues for adherence to natural laws since "the natur o' things doesn't change" (p. 113). He is an excellent carpenter and his work is part of his religion: "from very early days he saw clearly that carpentry was God's will" (p. 462). His religious views are essentially George Eliot's; he claims he will laugh at no man's religion but believes that our everyday lives are prayer as much as performing specifically religious ritual. Religion, says Adam, is "something else besides notions" (p. 173). Holloway points out, rightly I think, that the scene from which this quotation comes shows Adam Bede as George Eliot's "most deliberately created Authority. She even introduces him in total abstraction from the story to argue with his own creator about her characters and the problems they raise."[17]

Adam does indeed change during the course of the novel, but certain critics have, I think, exaggerated the degree of this change. Knoepflmacher's insistence that Adam has to learn that full humanity lies in man's distinction from nature[18] overlooks the fact that his two jobs, as carpenter, a worker with the wood nature has provided, and as the squire's controller of the woods, suggest that he already represents this distinction. It is also true that Adam is more compassionate initially than some critics allow; his loving support of his brother Seth is stressed throughout the novel.

If his conception of duty is a little hard and he tends to be conceited—"a little lifted up an' peppery-like" (p. 20)—his weaknesses are minor and no great transformation therefore takes place in him. He does not, as Hardy claims, have as much to learn as Lear:[19] he merely needs the rough edges planed a little by experience. His own suffering over Hetty and his father's death brings him to greater understanding, but it is an easy conversion and one, we suspect, that Adam would have eventually reached anyway. If it is intended as a "long and hard lesson" (p. 20), the novel does not dramatize it as such. What is more, Adam's rigidity is never in danger of harming anyone and is contrasted favorably with Arthur Donnithorne's softness. Adam may learn sympathy for others but he is throughout an idealized figure, the representative of George Eliot's values.

It is, therefore, difficult to see him as an example of that fallible humanity Dinah Morris accepts in place of her vocation as a Methodist evangelist. George Eliot seems to want us to accept a change in Dinah from a denier of the flesh, of the warm human emotions, to a girl willing to commit herself to life. She initally asks others to think of her as a saint; Seth Bede, her wrong suitor, considers her "too good an' holy for any man" (p. 35) and she tells him that marriage is not God's will for her. Like Dinah, Seth is a Methodist and they have other qualities in common; they "are striving after the same gifts" (p. 36), Dinah tells him. Seth's love is itself "hardly distinguishable from religious feeling" (p. 39) and he is always associated with doctrine and theory as opposed to Adam's individualism.

The problem with Dinah's conversion and subsequent marriage to Adam is that she appears so fully human when we see her as preacher. Her preaching is natural to her and her constant effort is towards alleviating other's pain, as we see in her behavior towards Hetty. We feel full sympathy for her in this early role and since she does not appear in the middle section of the novel, no gradual change can be dramatized. Suddenly, at the end, Dinah abruptly reverses her position and abandons her objection to being "enslaved to an earthly affection" (p. 480). She gives up preaching—it is convenient that the Methodist conference chooses this moment to forbid women to preach—and marries Adam.

George Eliot fulfills the convention by marrying hero and heroine as George Lewes suggested she should, but it does not work. In the terms set up in the novel, the union is by no means inevitable, and it is hard to find either Adam or Dinah convincing at the end. Dinah has adopted Adam's values, has settled for the small situation instead of trying to save the world, and it is not a satisfactory conclusion.

Maggie Tulliver, the heroine in The Mill on the Floss, is the first of George Eliot's sensitive and intelligent women frustrated by their environments. The Mill on the Floss has strong autobiographical elements which account, perhaps, for the authenticity of the early parts of the novel concerning Maggie and Tom Tulliver's childhood and for the vividness of the portraits of their relatives, most of whom play minor roles.

George Eliot's identification with Maggie, whose feelings are
obviously drawn from personal experience, has, as critics
have suggested, the potential for creating problems in the
novel.[20] Barbara Hardy, however, points out that "judgment is
passed, even though Maggie dies before she can achieve the
maturity which might accept and understand it."[21] In other
words, if this had not been a "wrong choice" treatment of the
two suitors convention, the problems that arise with Dorothea Brooke in *Middlemarch* might well have arisen here. As
it is, the two suitors convention in this form helps to solve
some of the difficulties implicit in George Eliot's treatment of
Maggie.

George Eliot described Maggie Tulliver in a letter to
Blackwood as "a character essentially noble but liable to great
error,"[22] but the novel itself expands this view of tragedy to
suggest an outlook that is Shakespearean rather than
Aristoltelian. Character is not the whole of our destiny:
"Hamlet, Prince of Denmark, was speculative and irresolute,
and we have a great tragedy in consequence. But if his father
had lived to a good old age, and his uncle had died an early
death, we can conceive Hamlet's having married Ophelia, and
got through life with a reputation of sanity, notwithstanding
many soliloquies . . ." (p. 351). Maggie's "great error" is to be
seen as the result of both her character and her environment.
The early chapters of the novel, which dramatize Maggie's
childhood at the Dorlcote Mill and in the surrounding War-
wickshire countryside, portray Maggie as a girl whose limited world provides no outlet for female intelligence.

She is brighter than her brother Tom, whom she idolizes,
and is described even by her father, who idolizes her, as "too
'cute for a woman" (p. 12). Maggie demonstrates her intelligence when, on a visit to his school, she masters Tom's
lessons far faster than he does. "I shall be a clever woman,"
Maggie says to her brother and receives a rebuke that
embodies the attitude of their society: "O I daresay, and a
nasty conceited thing. Everybody'll hate you" (p. 130). The
question of education dominates one section of the novel, and
George Eliot makes clear the faults of the prevailing system
which is as inadequate to the needs of practical minded boys

like Tom as to those of intellectual girls. Mr. Stelling, clergyman turned schoolmaster, is the representative of the system. He is unwilling to make the material more palatable to Tom "by mixing it with smattering, extraneous information, such as is given to girls" (p. 125), who, he believes, are "quick and shallow" (p. 134). Maggie Tulliver acts throughout this section as a refutation of this view. George Eliot leaves no doubt that the failure to educate Maggie properly, in the widest sense, is a major contributing factor in what follows.

Maggie's drive towards independence and her objections to love as the sole source of satisfaction allowed to women—"I wish I could make myself a world outside it, as men do" (p. 361)—are the result of what Philip Wakem calls "her unsatisfied intelligence" (p. 158). She needs to be loved and to love because she needs to feel herself useful, but, more than this, she needs to find an answer that will make some sense of a life now made miserable by her father's financial loss and accident. Her frustrated intelligence develops a soul-hunger in Maggie and she turns to herself because there is no outside reality to satisfy it. She is, of course, vulnerable to the first answer that appears, a doctrine of self-sacrifice which she learns from Thomas à Kempis. She forms plans of self-abnegation and "in the ardour of first discovery, renunciation seemed to her the entrance into that satisfaction which she had so long been craving in vain" (p. 255).

The attractions of this path for Maggie are clear enough. First, it is romantic and self-dramatizing: "her own life was still a drama for her, in which she demanded of herself that her part should be played with intensity" (p. 256). Second, she can do it for herself, "without the help of outward things" (p. 254). Third, it is within the bounds of virtuous activity allowed to females and she therefore does not have to be a clever woman whom nobody will like. She can simultaneously be independent and avoid annoying her brother Tom whose approval has always been of major importance in Maggie's life. Tom has constantly criticized her independent stands. He never questions male superiority and wants to do Maggie's thinking for her. She selects the one path which will meet his requirements and fulfill some of her own; indeed it is the path, though divested of its religious overtones, which Tom chooses for himself later in the novel.

The error in Maggie's choice of renunciation is clearly seen by Philip Wakem, crippled son of Mr. Tulliver's bitter enemy, schoolfellow of Tom and right suitor to Maggie. Philip wishes to provide some satisfaction for Maggie's mind. Since he believes that later "every rational satisfaction of your nature that you deny now, will assult you like a savage appetite" (p. 288), he attempts to dissuade Maggie from renunciation, particularly from renouncing her secret meetings with him in Red Deeps. Philip has genuine insight into Maggie's nature for, in contrast to Maggie, he has an almost painfully acute awareness of the real world. He is both artistic and sensitive, qualities which, if we remember George Eliot's view of the function of art as an enlarger of sympathies, are to her natural partners. He tells Maggie he hungers after what is "beautiful and good" (p. 264) and calls her to a shared delight in the beauties of life which cannot be obtained without the pain that reality must inevitably bring. He shows compassion even to those who injure him, to Tom when he injures his leg at school, to Maggie after her escapade with Stephen Guest.

His deformity may suggest Philip is George Eliot's example of the flawed human being, but he is nevertheless her spokesman. His voice against Maggie's renunciation as "an escape from pain" (p. 361) is clearly George Eliot's own. Barbara Hardy calls him, rightly I think, George Eliot's "most successful mentor and rescuer."[23] Maggie herself recognizes his function in her life, saying to him, "I had need have you always to find fault with me and teach me" (p. 362) and to Lucy later, "I would choose to marry him. I think it would be the best and highest lot for me" (p. 384). Joan Bennett is surely wrong when she claims that Maggie is drawn to Philip for the same reasons that Dorothea Brooke is drawn to Casaubon in *Middlemarch*.[24] Maggie does not romanticize Philip; their relationship is based on openness, trust, and common interests. It is Maggie's misfortune that she cannot love him enough to resist the temptations of the wrong suitor, Stephen Guest.

Stephen Guest, son of the owner of the largest oil mill in St. Ogg's, is tacitly engaged to Maggie's cousin Lucy Deane, in whose house she meets him. As Haight points out, Stephen has been harshly treated by critics from the beginning—"a mere hair-dressers block" Leslie Stephen calls him[25]—but in spite of some critical opinion to the contrary,[26] George Eliot hardly appears to view him more favorably. Philip comments directly upon Stephen's shallowness in his final letter to Maggie: "I have felt the vibration of chords in your nature that I have continually felt the want of in his" (p. 439). From the ironic introductory description of him as a dandy, whose learning is superficial, whose attachment to Lucy is based primarily on a concern for suitability and appearance, George Eliot's attitude to him is surely clear.[27]

This does not mean, however, that Maggie's attraction to him is not credible. It has been carefully prepared for, particularly through Philip, who warned her that repression of all feeling might lead to a violent outburst later. Stephen is the representative of the romanticized, self-dramatizing qualities which Maggie finds it so hard to conquer in herself. He is her idea of a figure out of Byron or Scott, whose poems she loves. What is more, he is the representative of the world of financial success which her brother Tom so much admires and which Philip wants no part of.

The problem with the ending of *The Mill on the Floss* is not in the character of Stephen but in the moral ambiguity of Maggie's choice. Maggie does not choose the wrong suitor; she half chooses him. Absentminded as the child who forgot her brother's rabbits, in a dreamlike state, she drifts down the river in the boat with Stephen until it is too late to return. Having revealed their love and so hurt both Philip and Lucy, Maggie refuses to marry Stephen and thus hurts him too. If one's criterion is supposed to be duty to the feelings of others, it is, as Haight says, hard to see how this refusal helps the situation.[28] Even if Maggie's refusal is a refutation of Darwin through the rejection of Stephen's appeal to the natural—and there is ample evidence for this in the novel[29]—it is thematically unsatisfactory in other ways. Maggie's renunciation resembles too closely the delight in renunciation for its own sake which has been condemned by George Eliot earlier in the novel.

Nevertheless, if one grants that Maggie is indeed guilty and cannot repair the damage she has caused, the final drowning sequence has a certain rightness. The boat ride in the flood, itself suggesting uncontrolled passion, echoes the mood of the earlier boat ride with Stephen. In both Maggie is paralyzed in a dreamlike state, and has no "distinct conception of her position" (p. 452); in both she experiences a cessation of struggle, a sense of being carried along against her will. The ending which reunites Maggie and Tom in death, though verging on melodrama, can nevertheless be read as a restitution—the only one Maggie can make—for the other loves she has shattered.

Maggie's maturity is a problem in this novel, as I have suggested; it is hard to accept her renunciation in the name of duty as necessary or ethically sound. The two suitors convention, however, presents no problems; indeed, since it is the wrong choice formula George Eliot uses, the convention here serves rather to alleviate the problems raised by Maggie's life after the incident with Stephen by making them irrelevant.

There are three women in Middlemarch whose development is shown in terms of the two suitors convention. Dorothea Brooke, who after suffering for choosing the wrong suitor, Casaubon, marries the right suitor Will Ladislaw, is one of the few heroines in the nineteenth-century fiction allowed to go on to happiness after the wrong choice. Mary Garth chooses Fred Vincy over the Reverend Farebrother. Rosamund Vincy marries Tertius Lydgate, lives to regret it, and briefly seeks a solution with Will Ladislaw, in a fashion which a contemporary novel might have developed into the bored-housewife-seeks-freedom-through-lover pattern of the convention. Only Dorothea Brooke, however, is central to the narrative, a centrality she shares with Lydgate, whose story *Middlemarch* was originally intended to be.

As Barbara Hardy suggests, the integration of George Eliot's earlier project *Miss Brooke* with Lydgate's story affects our response to Dorothea's: "Any suggestion of a feminist moral is controlled and extended by the complex plot, which puts Dorothea in her place as an example less of a feminine problem than of the frustrations of the human condition."[30] Certainly, the breadth of the canvas of *Middlemarch* is one of its great strengths. Our response to every theme, every situation, is qualified by the echoes of it or contrasts to it that the novel provides. This is the reason that the two suitors convention, which fails in Dorothea's case, does not do more damage to *Middlemarch*. The marriage of Dorothea and Will Ladislaw does not have to stand alone as the ending of the novel; other plot lines are also brought to resolution, and, although it is true that George Eliot amply demonstrates the interdependence of these lines, it is also true that each draws some degree of emphasis from the others.

However, Barbara Hardy surely underestimates the feminist elements of this novel. The situation of and attitudes toward women are frequently referred to; in fact these comments act as a sort of refrain, particularly in the earlier part of the novel when we are forming our view of Dorothea. Sir James Chettam's traditional view of the sexes is one of the few aspects of his otherwise sympathetic character which is treated satirically by George Eliot: "A man's mind—what there is of it—has always the advantage of being masculine... and even his ignorance is of a sounder quality."[31] His view is comparable to Mr. Brooke's "there is a lightness about the feminine mind" (p. 48) and to Mrs. Garth's belief that the female sex "was framed to be entirely subordinate" (p. 179). It is this attitude which allows Standish, Bulstrode and Chichely to discuss Rosamund Vincy as if she is a prize cow.

What is more, the plot makes the limited traditional view of women at least partly responsible for the difficulties the characters experience. Lydgate's view of women is seen to be largely responsible for the problems that beset him later. He considers "it one of the prettiest attitudes of the feminine mind to admire a man's pre-eminence without too precise a knowledge of what it consisted in" (p. 197). He selects Rosamund precisely because she is shallow, appears to worship him, but does not have any understanding of what matters to him; he relies on "the innate submission of the goose" (p. 261). It is hardly surprising that the marriage cannot stand the test of adversity. Both bad marriages in the novel—Dorothea's to Casaubon and Lydgate's to Rosamund—fail, at least in part, because of the traditional male view of women. It is important to note, though, that they are also undertaken for the wrong reasons by the women, whose situation in nineteenth-century society has demanded that they find satisfaction for their ambitions through men.

Although it may be true that the concentration of the prologue on Dorothea Brooke misleads us somewhat about the emphasis of the novel, it cannot be overlooked that it initially focuses our interest on her. In the prologue's well-known comparison between Dorothea and St. Theresa, the impossibility of Dorothea's satisfaction is clearly blamed on her situation. "A passionate, ideal nature" demands "an epic life"; "a certain spiritual grandeur" is "ill matched with the meanness of opportunity" (p. 3) provided for women in nineteenth-century England. George Eliot emphasizes that the problem is Dorothea's sex: "if there were one level of feminine incompetence as strict as the ability to count to three and no more, the social lot of women might be treated with scientific certitude" (p. 4). In spite of the irony to which some of Dorothea's attitudes are later subjected—and there is much—this view of her as a person essentially too noble and ardent for her situation remains.

Dorothea is in many ways like Maggie Tulliver; she has her unworldly cleverness and yearns for "some lofty conception of the world" which would have "intensity and greatness" (p. 6) and might lead her to martyrdom. Like Maggie, she seeks the answer, the key to life, "a binding theory which could bring her own life and doctrine into strict connection with that amazing past" (p. 63). The best she can achieve in useful action is planning cottages for the poor of Tipton. Like Maggie, she is given to renunciation and rejects fine clothes and her mother's jewelry. George Eliot points out at once the innate selfishness of her self-abnegation, telling us that Dorothea looked forward to renouncing her riding because "she felt she enjoyed it in a pagan sensuous way" (p. 7). Her own desire to see herself as good is greater than her concern for others; she catches herself regretting the prosperity of

Lowick which will leave her little to do in the parish as Casaubon's wife. She is guilty of the same self-centeredness as Maggie Tulliver and for the same reason: her education— "that toy-box history of the world adapted to young ladies" (p. 63)—has failed her.

As Bernard Paris states, "her subjective approach to Casaubon was not the result of a basically egoistic nature; it was the product rather of her frustration."[32] In the passage in which George Eliot analyzes Dorothea's reasons for marrying Casaubon, she emphasizes once more the inadequacies of Dorothea's education. A girl who had a great thirst for knowledge and had experienced only "the nibblings and judgments of a discursive mouse" (pp 20-21), might well think that marrying the scholarly clergyman Casaubon "would be like marrying Pascal" (p. 21). She visualizes her husband teaching her Latin, Greek, and perhaps Hebrew so that she can help him in his work. Marriage to Casaubon is the only outlet offered for her curious mind: " . . . what lamp was there but knowledge? Surely learned men kept the only oil; and who more learned than Mr. Casaubon?" (p. 64). Of course, Dorothea's willingness to satisfy her ambitions through any man is a second best choice. Like so many women of her generation, and a few in ours, she has been taught that glory for a woman was to be a reflected beam of her husband's. Nevertheless, George Eliot sympathetically tells us Dorothea "had not reached that point of renunciation at which she would have been satisfied with having a wise husband: she wished, poor child, to be wise herself" (p. 47).

If it is hardly within Dorothea's power to recognize immediately that Casaubon is no Pascal, she can be faulted, perhaps, for not imagining what might be wrong with marrying Pascal. Her sister, Celia, who shared the same environment, understands far better the possible problems for a young girl in a marriage to a bachelor old enough to be her father. If she could not see the errors in his work, Dorothea might have taken notice, as her sister did, of the way he drank his soup. This failure arises from her refusal to acknowledge the importance of feeling and of the physical which is her most striking weakness in the early part of the novel. Her professed disinterest in art is linked to her unawakened sensuality. Dorothea claims that she cannot see the beauty in paintings, and the intense grandeur of Rome shocks her Puritan sensibilities. George Eliot, however, makes us aware that Dorothea does not lack passion but is merely unawakened. Will Ladislaw, who thinks when he first meets her that "there could be no sort of passion in a girl who would marry Casaubon" (p. 59), is surprised by the sensuousness of her voice.

Dorothea has invented the Mr. Casaubon she marries, "seeing there in vague labyrinthine extension every quality she herself brought" (p. 17); she is not perceptive enough to recognize that he, too, is the center of his own world. She thinks of him as the great lamp-bearer, a man "who could illuminate principle with the widest knowledge" (p. 16). Images of illumination, used throughout the novel to suggest Dorothea's ideals, are attributed by her to Casaubon before the marriage: "All Dorothea's ideal passion was transfused through a mind struggling towards an ideal life; the radiance of her transfigured girlhood fell on the first object that came within its level" (p. 32). Ironically, as the metaphors here suggest, it is Dorothea, not Casaubon, who provides the illumination.

Casaubon is, of course, very different from the man Dorothea believes him to be. He has cemented himself in the faults Dorothea is to outgrow. His scholarly attempt to find the key to all mythologies is his equivalent to Dorothea's search for the one answer to life. He is the extreme example of an atrophied emotional life; when he fails to feel sufficiently for his young bride, he concludes "that the poets had much exaggerated the force of masculine passion" (p. 46). Sir James, who believes her uncle Mr. Brooke should try to stop this marriage, objects that Casaubon "has got no good red blood in his body" (p. 52).

Casaubon believes that women are gifted with "the capability of an ardent self-sacrificing affection" (p. 37) and should be subordinate to their husbands. Dorothea finds this self-sacrifice cold and unrewarding; Casaubon has little time for her even on their honeymoon and resists allowing her to help in his work. Ironically, it is the very intelligence she hoped to satisfy in this marriage that makes her perceive Casaubon's faults as a scholar. Half recognizing this, he turns further away from her in fear. Far from being a lamp-bearer, he is a wanderer in dark passages. His work is secondhand, having been superseded years ago by German scholars. Dorothea's refusal to complete his work after his death, after she has been providentially rescued from a deathbed promise to do so, marks her assertion of a spiritual independence. She writes on the tabulation he has left for her, "Do you not see now that I could not submit my soul to yours, by working hopelessly at what I have no belief in?" (p. 343).

The person who rescues Dorothea from the faults she shares with Casaubon and brings her to acceptance of his own virtues is Casaubon's young cousin, Will Ladislaw, the right suitor. Barbara Hardy correctly points out that the portrait of Dorothea is exempted from irony once she marries Casaubon and that direct comment and romantic and ideal images create a sentimental bid for sympathy.[33] The irony directed at Dorothea's idealization of Casaubon is absent after his death. It is important to recognize this in evaluating the problems with this part of the two suitors convention.

Will Ladislaw, supposedly based on George Lewes, George Eliot's lover and companion for many years, is the opposite of Casaubon, who fears his insight. He is presented as a Romantic artist: he is first seen at any length mixing with the German artists at Rome. Mr. Brooke sees him as "a kind of Shelley" (p. 263); Mrs. Cadwallader as "a sort of Byronic hero" (p. 278). He is the advocate of the imaginative over the rational and believes "that there should be some unknown regions preserved as hunting-grounds for the poetic imagination" (p. 60). He even has a secret ancestry and describes himself as a rebel.

When Dorothea comes to know him, she turns to him for understanding because, like all artists in George Eliot's fiction, he has the capacity to see reality and is perceptive about others. This understanding of others as subjective realities he shares with Philip Wakem, whose kindness he equals. George Eliot, rather sentimentally, illustrates this in

Will's treatment of children and old ladies. Like Philip Wakem, Will believes "the best piety is to enjoy" (p. 163) and states his philosophy to Dorothea as "To love what is good and beautiful when I see it" (p. 287). Nevertheless, he seems more of a dilettante than Philip and is uncertain of his aims, drifting into one activity after another for unclear reasons. It is an impression of him which we form early and which is never quite shaken, though George Eliot clearly means us to take him as the representative of her values.

Will teaches Dorothea the religion of humanity, a duty to others based on feeling, for which the novel as a whole argues. Situation after situation illustrates this theme: Farebrother gives up Mary to Fred; Mrs. Bulstrode stands by Mr. Bulstrode in his disgrace; even Rosamund surrenders her own infatuation for Will Ladislaw and reveals his love to Dorothea. Will is the spokesman of these values, of "the deep-seated habit of direct fellow-feeling with individual fellow-men" (p. 453). Under his influence Dorothea begins to see Casaubon clearly, and only then finds herself capable of compassion for him. She helps Lydgate out of "human fellowship" and tries to help Rosamund. This desire to help, however, clearly marks a directing into a new channel of that "idea of some active good" (p. 557) which still "haunted her like a passion" (p. 557). She now visualizes the great deed on a personal level; theories, plans for cottages, the search for the one key to life have been abandoned, but she has retained her desire for heroism and George Eliot does not treat this ironically. Lydgate's comment that "This young creature has a heart large enough for the Virgin Mary" (p. 563) is not undercut.

One problem is that, as many critics have recognized, Will Ladislaw is hardly adequate to embody the virtues he supposedly represents. His actions in the name of human fellowship are not the equivalent of those other characters perform or, at least, are not so convincingly dramatized. Henry James points out that Ladislaw is "not the ideal foil to Mr. Casaubon which her soul must have imperiously demanded; and if the author of the 'Key to all Mythologies' sinned by lack of [ardor], Ladislaw too has not the concentrated fervor essential in the man chosen by so nobly strenuous a heroine."[34]

Thale stresses that the problem with Ladislaw is that he is not drawn fully enough,[35] and this is certainly one of the problems; we do not see his changes as growth in the way we do Fred Vincy's, for example.

The opponents of this view argue that Ladislaw is fallible and that this is George Eliot's point. Knoepflmacher claims that "By marrying the fallible Ladislaw, Dorothea admits her own needs as a woman, yet admits also the insufficiency of her abstracted ideals."[36] This argument is attractive because it solves the one major difficulty in an otherwise brillant novel; unfortunately it is not valid. Dorothea does not stop idealizing Will: she praises his virtues, his public speaking, his ability to explain clearly, his concern for the rest of the world (p. 395); he remains as "good as I had believed you to be" (p. 592). Most important, all the imagery of illumination and revelation associated with Dorothea's idealism is transferred to Will: "Here, with the nearness of an answering smile, here within the vibrating bond of mutual speech, was the bright creature whom she had trusted—who had come to her like the spirit of morning visiting the dim vault where she sat as the bride of a worn-out life" (p. 576). She is reunited with Will amid thunder and lightning.[37]

The structure and imagery of the novel argue for seeing this marriage as the fulfillment of Dorothea's dreams, but we have surely been invited to see Dorothea as having a nobility, an intensity, that should not have been satisfied by Will Ladislaw nor indeed by becoming a copy of anyone else. If we grant Will ideal status, the problem still remains. The major difficulty that can arise with the two suitors convention is illustrated here: Dorothea has accepted Will's values and there is therefore an element of subordination inconsistent with a view of maturity as spiritual independence. George Eliot makes it clear that Dorothea's search for the satisfaction of her ambitions through another's was wrong in the case of Casaubon yet wants us to accept it as right with Will Ladislaw. She has attacked the very premises of the convention which structures her novel, yet continues to use it.

Almost as if she saw the problems caused by the marriage of Will and Dorothea, George Eliot tries to temper the ending in the last few pages, returning to the notion of the impossibility of achieving an ideal life: "Certainly those determining acts of her life were not ideally beautiful. They were the mixed result of young and noble impulse struggling amidst the conditions of an imperfect social state" (p. 612). Commenting on her marriage to Ladislaw, George Eliot writes "Many who knew her, thought it a pity that so substantive and rare a creature should have been absorbed into the life of another" (p. 611). It is hard not to count oneself amongst them.

In *Daniel Deronda*, as in *Middlemarch*, comments on the situation of and attitude to women provide a kind of background music to the action. The rector of Pennicote sees his niece, Gwendolen Harleth, the heroine, as Mr. Brooke sees Dorothea. George Eliot comments sarcastically on his expectations for her marriage: "Why should he be expected to differ from his contemporaries in this matter, and wish his niece a worse end of her charming maidenhood than they would approve as the best possible."[35] More of the women in this novel than in any earlier one see their situation as unfair: young Kate Meyrick tells her mother, "I notice mothers are like the people I deal with—the girls' doings are always prized low" (p. 367); the Princess, Daniel's real mother, says to him, "You are not a woman. You may try—but you can never imagine what it is to have a man's force of genius in you, and yet to suffer the slavery of being a girl" (p. 474). Refusing to act the domestic angel—"But suppose *we* need that men should be better than we are" (p. 250)—Gwendolen Harleth finds herself at the beginning of the novel in the same situation as Dorothea Brooke and Maggie Tulliver. She had had an inadequate education and sees no outlet for her abilities.

Nevertheless, in tone *Daniel Deronda* is a very different novel from *Middlemarch*. Jerome Thale points out that in *Daniel Deronda* we are struck by the darkness of the moral vision,[39] a fact which he associates with the greater intellectual pessimism of later nineteenth-century England. Certainly the novel contains characters—Grandcourt, Gwendolen's husband, and his assistant Lush in particular—who are unredeemably evil; Gwendolen herself seems to suffer from an existential *angst* as much as from a frustrated intellect and experiences moments of spiritual dread which create a sinister atmosphere unknown in the earlier novels. Evil here is a positive force to be battled, not merely the absence of good; when Grandcourt is described as feeling that "In some form or other the Furies had crossed his threshold" (p. 268), George Eliot is not merely using a metaphor.

In other ways, too, *Daniel Deronda* differs from *Middlemarch*. Writing in 1877, Edmund Dowden said, "Whether consciously so designed or not, *Daniel Deronda* comes to us as a counterpoise or a correlative of the work which immediately preceded it."[40] For the first time George Eliot does not make an argument for compromise; the title character of this novel is allowed fulfillment of his vision. The counterpart of Dorothea, Maggie, Esther, and Diana is a man, Daniel Deronda, who is brought up by and imagines himself the illegitimate son of Sir Hugo Mallinger. Perhaps because he is a man, Daniel achieves the great purpose the women cannot; he does not have to settle for small deeds. His is a search for identity like Esther Lyon's, a search which leads him to recognition and acceptance of his Jewishness and discovery of a Zionist mission.

Almost without exception critics see the Daniel part of the novel—and in spite of the yoking together of the plots, the novel does split into two parts—as a failure. Some stress, as Thale does, that the failure lies in George Eliot's inadequate and uncritical knowledge of Zionism.[41] The characterization of Daniel fails also for basic novelistic reasons which transcend those connected with George Eliot's idealized right suitors. Mr. Fraser's opinion of him is unfortunately borne out by the novel: Daniel "was continually seen in acts of considerateness that struck his companions as moral eccentricity" (p. 132). Obviously his kindness to Gwendolen in returning her necklace and to Mirah in saving her life, his understanding of Gwendolen's suffering, his ability "to feel strongly" and "to question actively" (p. 382) are admirable. However, Daniel has a tone of moral superiority which is not likable. We never see him perform an action which does not illustrate his moral worth and George Eliot's moral scheme. He is a static, flat character; he does not grow spiritually as he seeks his mission in life, but is an idealized figure from the beginning. As Leavis says, "we are to take him as the beau ideal of masculinity." (XVI).

Like Felix Holt and to some extent Adam Bede, Daniel is too didactic, especially in his function as spiritual guide and mentor to Gwendolen Harleth. She turns to him in a "precipitancy of confidence" (p. 334) which is not entirely credible, and he acts as her conscience from the moment she sees him gazing at her across the casino like "an evil eye" (p. 4). When she talks to Grandcourt with Deronda in the room, she feels his face expresses an unfavorable judgment on her standards and she resents his influence on her. As she changes, she begins to see "all her acts through the impression they would make on Deronda" (p. 507) and the evil eye becomes "a terrible-browed angel." Finally, she attributes what goodness she has achieved to him: "If you had not been good, I should have been more wicked than I am" (p. 529).

The relationship between Gwendolen and Daniel is saved to some extent because he is not her lover. Since in the early stages of their relationship Gwendolen is married to Grandcourt and in the later Daniel is in love with Mirah, circumstances prevent what is in many ways a mutual attraction from going beyond friendship. Daniel fulfills all the functions of the right suitor, embodies the virtues the heroine is to learn and helps her to reach them, but the final marriage is avoided. This does not redeem the Deronda part of the novel, but it does to some extent rescue Gwendolen's story from the trap into which Dorothea's falls.

The Gwendolen Harleth story, which dominates the first half of the novel, is its richest section. When she first appears, Gwendolen combines the intelligence and drive of a Dorothea with the shallowness of soul of a Hetty Sorrel. Because George Eliot does not share her values, she is able to resist what Leavis calls "any tempting opportunity for insidious self-identification" (xix). For this reason, Gwendolyn does seem finally to transcend her destiny.

She is presented as a conceited girl who has "a sense of superior claims" (p. 8) and is continually bored with what life offers her. She has a command, a presence, a combination of beauty and physical grace, which draws attention to her and makes even her mother treat her as "a queen in exile" (p. 28). She has a strong will, insisting on her own comfort even to the extent of refusing to fetch her mother's painkilling medicine in the middle of the night. There is a suggestion of evil in Gwendolen that the thoughtless Hetty Sorrel lacked; it manifests itself early in such violent acts as the strangling of her sister's canary.

Whereas Dorothea is unawakened, Gwendolen really lacks passion. When her cousin Rex Gascoigne, an early suitor who is not central to the novel, tries to make love to her, she objects "with a sort of physical repulsion, to being directly made love to" (p. 49). When she is engaged to Grandcourt and this usually undemonstrative man kisses her neck, she pulls away with "marked agitation" (p. 242). Hunting imagery supports this notion of Gwendolen as the goddess Diana. Thale believes, probably correctly, that part of her revulsion to the knowledge that Grandcourt has kept a mistress for nine years is the realization that the man she is to marry is "sexually menacing."[42] This inadequacy in Gwendolen is related to a general coldness of spirit; nothing is worth living for, she tells her mother, because she is incapable of loving anybody.

In spite of her fear of sexuality, Gwendolen is finally forced to attempt to satisfy her ambitions through marriage, though she initially yearns for success outside it. She sees marriage as dull and humdrum; she does not "wish to lead the same sort of life as ordinary young ladies did" (p. 37) and envisions going to the North Pole, riding in steeplechases or "being a queen in the East like Lady Hester Stanhope" (p. 49). When it becomes apparent that Grandcourt will propose, she plans to reject him or, at the very least, to have control of him: "If she chose to take this husband, she would have him know that she was not going to renounce her freedom" (p. 96).

Breaking her promise to Mrs. Glasher, his mistress who still hopes he will marry her, Gwendolen finally accepts Grandcourt, the wrong suitor but a wealthy landowner who can rescue her family from financial distress. She finds him tolerable before marriage because he is "quiet and free from absurdities" (p. 100). She lacks the perception and perhaps the opportunity to recognize that Grandcourt has all her own weaknesses in an extreme form. He is the only wrong suitor in George Eliot's fiction whom she presents entirely without sympathy; he has no redeeming qualities. Gwendolen marries believing Grandcourt "a man over whom she was going to have indefinite power" (p. 233). However, he is an expert in wielding power and enjoys it as much as she does: "He meant to be master of a woman who would have liked to master him" (p. 237); he was "not jealous of anything unless it threatened his mastery" (p. 241). Gwendolen discovers that he has "a will like that of a crab or a boa-constrictor" (p. 317) and "a surprising acuteness in detecting that situation of feeling in Gwendolen which made her proud and rebellious spirit dumb and helpless before him" (p. 318). Ironically, as an exercise of his will he forces her to go on the boating trip that causes his own death.

As well as her desire for power, Grandcourt shares Gwendolen's love of danger and her emphasis on appearance. He objects to her concentration on Deronda in public not out of jealousy but because it is unbecoming in his wife. He is colder than Gwendolen could conceive of being, as is demonstrated in his treatment of Mrs. Glasher and later of Gwendolen herself. Lydia Glasher's letter to Gwendolen on her marriage tells her correctly that Grandcourt "has a withered heart" (p. 267). His conceit is impenetrable by any notion that a woman could find him morally repugnant.

This is, however, just what Gwendolen begins to find him under the suffering her marriage brings. She gradually begins to change, a change which is revealed chiefly in conversations with Deronda. She admits her selfishness and begins to act more generously towards her mother and sisters. She has "a root of conscience in her" (p. 503) and she recognizes that her marriage pact with Grandcourt was like selling her soul to the devil; she has sold "her truthfulness and sense of justice" (p. 504). She wills Grandcourt's death and, when he is accidently drowned, feels she has caused it. It is the recognition of the will to destroy in herself and her desire to conquer it that truly begins Gwendolen's spiritual rehabilitation. Driven by guilt, she confesses to Daniel, voicing a desire for goodness, and he provides her with the vision of a life of atonement: "You can, you will, be among the best of women, such as make others glad that they were born" (p. 580). Her first act of renunciation has to be acceptance of Daniel's separation from her and we leave Gwendolen looking forward optimistically to an undefined future: "She was for the first time being dislodged from her supremacy in her own world, and getting a sense that her horizon was but a dipping onward of an existence with which her own was revolving" (p. 607).

Gwendolen's life of rununciation is somehow acceptable in a way that Maggie Tulliver's is not. This is perhaps because of our sense of Gwendolen's greater guilt or because we have never been encouraged to find her admirable or to identify with her ambitions. We are never asked to accept her as mature, merely as having taken the first step on the road to maturity; in her final letter to Daniel, she says she accepts the possibility of making "others glad that they were born" but does "not yet see how that can be" (p. 611). The didactic nature of Daniel's part in the two suitors convention is troublesome in this novel and certainly Gwendolen's development is shown entirely through her relationship with men. Nevertheless, the open ending is an improvement; Gwendolen is left "in the isolation of a new beginning"[43] which could, theoretically at least, lead her beyond Daniel into independent spiritual adventures she cannot yet dream of.

In spite of the many variations of the two suitors convention which George Eliot employs and the varying success she achieves with it, two problems constantly recur in her fiction. The first is the problem of the idealization of the right suitor— Adam Bede, Felix Holt and Daniel Deronda—which, as well as creating the usual fictional difficulties inherent in idealized characters, is in direct conflict with George Eliot's own stated aim of showing us the ordinariness of men and women. The heroine who has to learn this all too often learns it about everyone but the right suitor.

The second problem is more complex and concerns the heroine herself. George Eliot's women are frequently women of great stature who dominate the stage they act on, and

George Eliot encourages our identification with them both by portraying their ideals sympathetically and by illustrating the narrowness of their situations. This is true of Maggie Tulliver, of Dorothea Brooke, of Dinah Morris, and to some extent of Esther Lyon. Although we may accept intellectually that life is a compromise and small deeds can be important, we are unwilling, I think, to see these women reduced to being wives who waddle. Maggie's death at least is dramatic enough for the expectations she has aroused. It is hard to say what ending would have been more adequate than marriage to the right suitor for these heroines—the ending of *Daniel Deronda* perhaps opens up possibilities—but nevertheless the greatness of their problem seems to demand a larger solution. In the words Henry James uses of Felix Holt, it is difficult to accept these heroines as "only 'utterly married'; which is all very well in its place, but which by itself makes no conclusion."[44]

Chapter Six

Her Transitory Self

THE FOUR NOVELS discussed in this chapter differ from those considered earlier in two main respects: they all have feminism or "the woman question" as their central concern; all clearly and directly define female maturity in terms of being oneself, of developing an individual identity. It is significant, of course, that these novelists have a greater perspective on the nineteenth century and can, therefore, identify a specifically Victorian attitude to women. They all openly reject this Victorian concept of the lady as implicitly medieval, based upon courtly love traditions which are no longer viable in a more modern world. All argue for the position Forster takes in *A Room with a View:* "Men, declaring that she inspires them to it, move joyfully over the surface, having the most delightful meetings with other men, happy, not because they are masculine, but because they are alive. Before the show breaks up she would like to drop the august title of the Eternal Woman, and go there as her transitory self."[1]

In three of the novels, George Meredith's *The Egoist* (1877), E.M. Forster's *A Room with a View* (1908), and H.G. Wells's *Ann Veronica* (1909), this concept of female maturity is clearly in conflict with the use of the two suitors convention. The fourth, George Gissing's *The Odd Women* (1892), is included because it faces one of the problems which has haunted this study: to what extent is any marriage possible in nineteenth-century society for a woman who really wishes to be an individual in her own right? In facing this question,

Gissing comes to terms, perhaps unintentionally, with the problems of the two suitors convention.

In choosing *The Egoist* I do not mean to suggest that other Meredith novels are not relevant to my discussion; *Diana of the Crossways,* in particular, is interesting in this regard. The question of marriage and its relation to a woman's identity is, after all, central to all of Meredith's work.[2] But *The Egoist* is frequently praised as the most "beautifully planned"[3] of Meredith's novels and the problem of the two suitors convention is basically a structural problem. In addition, its heroine, Clara Middleton, makes a convenient comparison with Jane Austen's heroines with whom this study began; she does, as Karl states, resemble Elizabeth Bennet, and *The Egoist* is a comedy of manners as intricate as *Pride and Prejudice.*

In spite of these resemblances to Jane Austen's fiction, *The Egoist* is in many ways an unconventional novel. As Gillian Beer points out, Meredith engages "the ideal hero of popular Victorian fiction," Sir Willoughby Patterne, to the pure and pretty "typical novel heroine," Clara Middleton, prepares for a conventional courtship and wedding, and then "takes the easy expectations of society and plot judgments of fiction and turns them askew."[5] It is precisely the unconventional nature of Meredith's treatment and the depth of his insight into the psychological truths about many marriage relationships that make his failure to achieve the final reversal and reject the two suitors convention all the more striking.

Meredith takes the story on the willow pattern plate for his model.[6] Dr. Middleton, a widower like the mandarin in the willow pattern tale, plans to marry his daughter, Clara, to a wealthy suitor, Sir Willoughby Patterne, representative of the established order and of the established attitude towards women. She, however, prefers a poor but honorable man, Vernon Whitford, who in the original was her father's secretary and in the novel works for Sir Willoughby. In the willow pattern story the heroine and the secretary escape by changing into birds; Clara and Vernon go climbing in the Alps. The problem with the two suitors convention is not so much that Clara marries—Walter Wright has made a strong argument that, in terms of Meredith's views, marriage for Clara is not necessarily impossible[7]—but that she marries Vernon Whitford. Vernon leads the way throughout the novel; Clara merely echoes his actions and develops in his mold. At the end of the novel, she has become Vernon, not herself.

Sir Willoughby Patterne, the egoist of the title, is "fifth in descent from Simon Patterne of Patterne Hall,"[8] the perfect image of a young squire, as his name suggests, and adored by those around him. John Goode calls him "the very essence of the social structure"[9] in an article which argues that Willoughby's egoism has to be preserved because it is the basis of an ordered society. It is dangerous, however, to push this argument too far. It misplaces the emphasis of the book which, although it allows some sympathy for Willoughby later, holds his complacency up to ridicule and firmly establishes him as the wrong suitor.

Willoughby accepts society's view of him, adores himself as much as he is adored, and thus treats himself as an object of worship. Two early scenes define him: one in which he attempts to adopt Lieutenant Crossjay Patterne, a remote member of his family, and subsequently rejects him for failing to live up to the image of a gallant marine who might add color to Willoughby's entourage; another in which he is jilted by his first fianceé, Constantia Durham, and is only concerned about his own pride, about how he will appear to the world. Appearance, too, is his chief reason for selecting his second fianceé, Clara Middleton: "Clara was young, healthy, handsome; she was therefore fitted to be his wife, the mother of his children, his companion picture.... She completed him, added the softer lines wanting to his portrait before the world" (p. 46).

His egotism blinds him. Other people are objects not subjects to him and so when Clara gradually begins to see through him and wants to break the engagement, he can see it only as her jealousy, the explanation most flattering to himself. Clara is really in rebellion against his ownership of her: Willoughby feels he owns even his friends—"He likes his friends about him" (p. 239) is Dr. Middleton's generous explanation of this—and toward Clara his possessiveness is suitably stronger. Women have no identities to him, and thus can be created by their husbands: "He desired to shape her character to the feminine of his own and betrayed the surprise of a slight disappointment at her advocacy of her ideas" (p. 49). He talks of himself to her as "the possessor of the whole of you! Your thoughts, hopes, all" (p. 86). He intends her to have contact with the world only through him.

Willoughby's view of women is, of course, Ruskin's, the established view of women as angels to be worshiped, which denies their humanity. Meredith clearly sides with Clara in rejecting this view. "Women," says Willoughby, "must teach us to venerate them" (p. 55). The possibility of "women of mixed essences shading off the divine to the considerably lower" (p. 110) is beyond his understanding. "His notion of women was the primitive black and white: there are good women, bad women" (p. 109).

It is clear enough why this view, and its holder with it, are rejected by Clara, but in the name of what personal goal does this rejection take place? When she first appears in the novel, she is naive, "the true ideal, fresh-gathered morning fruit in a basket" (p. 44); she appears to be going to follow the usual path of a novel heroine towards maturity and marriage. She has already agreed to marry Willoughby, has done the expected thing, has "acquiesce(d) in the principle of selection" (p. 43). In her concern for the customary thing, duty, she resembles the wrong suitor, Willoughby; she even describes herself to Laetitia Dale as an egoist, "thinking of no one but myself, scheming to make use of every soul I meet" (p. 157). Looking back at the end of the novel, Clara says once more "I was the Egoist" (p. 481). Some form of egoism is, of course, necessary for Clara to succeed at all; she has to learn to assert herself, to take her freedom herself, rather than use others to gain her ends. "A parasite and a chalice" (p. 47) who comes to see most marriages as slavery, the bride as "a bondwoman" (p. 63), and who argues for equality with men, cannot change her condition by depending on one man to rescue her from bondage to another.

Clara asserts the right to her own mind, "married or not" (p. 78); she cries "I love my liberty. I want to be free" (p. 107); she is shocked when young Crossjay, Vernon's pupil, says to her

"But, Miss Middleton, when you're married you won't be Clara Middleton" (p. 243). Clara's goal is to be an individual, to have a distinct identity, to relate to the world in her own right: "she would not . . . by love's transmutation, literally be the man she was to marry. She preferred to be herself, with the egoism of women! She said it. She said: 'I must be myself to be of any value to you, Willoughby'" (p. 50). It is a goal Meredith obviously approves. Vernon Whitford tells her how to achieve it: "she was to do everything for herself, do and dare everything, decide upon everything. He told her flatly that so would she learn to know her own mind, and flatly that it was her penance" (p. 199).

Here is the problem with the novel. The right suitor, Vernon Whitford, not only tells Clara what to do but he foreshadows and guides her every act. She even strides along at his side, keeping pace with him. But he is not merely her comrade, though Meredith would obviously like us to believe this in order to accept the notion of an ideal shared, open marriage at the end. Early on Vernon tells Clara that her willingness to challenge authority makes her a fit "Alpine comrade" (p. 118). Vernon is the suitor who embodies the right virtues and Clara has to learn from him, to follow him.

Vernon is a scholar, described by Dr. Middleton as "clever and simple" (p. 67). He is Willoughby's opposite and is frequently contrasted with him. Karl calls Vernon "a true synthesis of Blood and Brain,"[10] and he is frequently seen out of doors, stretched out, reading, under the wild cherry tree or climbing in the Alps. Vernon Whitford, Clara realizes stands "for the world taken into her confidence" (p. 106), the world that Willoughby wished to keep from her. He is her conscience as Daniel Deronda is Gwendolen Harleth's: "a scrutiny . . . though his eyes did but rest on her a second or two, signified that he read her line by line and to the end" (p. 102). He rejects submission to Willoughby before Clara does and she follows the path he has laid out, even learning to accept the natural impulses in herself and to cry out her wretchedness. "It is the cry of an animal!" (p. 405) her father says to her in horror. Vernon guides her directly, not merely by example, and, while claiming detachment, leads her to reject Willoughby and ultimately to accept himself.

The problem is not merely that Vernon Whitford is a rather weak and unsatisfactory right suitor—Angus Wilson calls him depressing[11]—it is that Clara's attainment of her individuality is described entirely in terms of her gradual approximation of Vernon's virtues. Thus the structure of the novel in terms of the two suitors convention is clearly in conflict with the expressed views on female maturity. As John Goode says, "Considering how much she has to rely on men, on Crossjay, on De Craye, on Vernon, it is ironic that feminists found it cheering."[12]

Forster described *A Room with a View*, somewhat ambiguously, as his "nicest" novel,[13] and in many ways it is. It is unashamedly and innocently romantic, concluding with an affirmation quite different from the qualified ending of such later Forster novels as *Howards End* and *A Passage to India*. Calvin Bedient calls it "an unguarded celebration of desire" in which "Instinct is 'reality,' desire is 'holy.'"[14] It is the story of a young English girl, Lucy Honeychurch, who falls in love with a young man, George Emerson, in Italy, takes the rest of the book to admit she loves him, and then marries him. In spite of a vague sense that the Greece she does not visit somehow represents grander opportunities than the Italy she does and in spite of Forster's own comments fifty years later that George and Lucy did not live entirely happily ever after,[15] *A Room with a View* ends like a fairy tale with the implication that perfection has been achieved, all problems resolved: "Youth enwrapped them; the song of Phaethon announced passion requited, love attained" (p. 246).

The problem of the novel, as Forster presents it, is Lucy's problem: she must learn to stop living by social lies and find her true self; in other words, she must attain maturity in a form not perceptibly different from the way Meredith defines it for Clara Middleton. For the reader the problem with *A Room with a View* is related to but goes beyond Lucy's problem. Lucy's maturing is described in terms of the two suitors convention: the values of Cecil Vyse, the wrong suitor, must be rejected; those of George Emerson, the right suitor, emulated and finally adopted. But the most important of the right values in this novel is mental and spiritual independence, a value which inevitably conflicts with the two suitors convention. Thus in *A Room with a View*, as in *The Egoist*, the right ending aesthetically is the wrong ending thematically.

When Lucy Honeychurch first arrives in Florence with her chaperone, Cousin Charlotte, she is on her way to becoming the embodiment of the Victorian definition of a lady; she has been taught to value tact, gentility, "niceness," to live at second hand. This is the attitude represented by Cousin Charlotte, who fastens her window shutters against the world and who practices apparent self-denial, which is itself a form of selfishness. Charlotte explains to Lucy why most things are unladylike: "It was not that ladies were inferior to men; it was that they were different. Their mission was to inspire others to achievement rather than to achieve themselves. Indirectly, by means of tact and a spotless name, a lady could accomplish much" (p. 46). Lucy has not, up to this point, experienced life directly. She even intends to experience Florence by means of other people's information, has learned the most important dates of Florentine History, extending "uncritical approval to every well-known name" (p. 48). This is the view of a suitable life for women that Meredith's Willoughby holds and, like Meredith, Forster disapproves of it: "There is much that is immortal in this medieval lady. The dragons have gone, and so have the knights, but still she lingers in our midst. . . . But alas! the creature grows degenerate. In her heart also there are springing up strange desires. She too is enamoured of heavy winds, and vast panoramas, and the green expanses of the sea" (p. 47).

We know, of course, early on that Lucy will escape the destiny of Cousin Charlotte. Her music is one clue; musical ability, as always in Forster, designates those on the side of the angels. When Lucy plays the piano, she is "no longer either a rebel or a slave" (p. 34), Forster tells us; she plays "on the side of Victory" (p. 35) and reveals a greater capacity for direct experience than she has so far demonstrated. Mr. Beebe remarks that one day "The water-tight compartments in her will break down, and music and life will mingle. Then we shall have her heroically good, heroically bad" (p. 106).

The other clue is her response to the Emersons, father and

son, whom she is lucky enough to meet at the Pension Bertolini. As their name suggests, they represent the virtues of honesty, immediate experience, and self-reliance and are associated throughout with nature and expansive views. It is their offer of rooms with views—an offer Charlotte wishes to reject—that first draws Lucy to them. Old Mr. Emerson, Forster's representative, delivers the lectures in the novel, arguing for the rights of babies over churches which stultify growth, for directness instead of tact, for what is natural rather than what is civilized, for a world in which men and women will be comrades. We shall enter this world, he believes, "when we no longer despise our bodies" (p. 146). By giving the right suitor, George Emerson, a father who can lecture the heroine for him, Forster solves the problem of creating an overly didactic right suitor.

In Florence Lucy gradually changes: "instead of acquiring information, she began to be happy" (p. 24). A significant experience in bringing about this change is her observation of a street fight and a killing when she is with George Emerson. Forster uses this scene to suggest the greater value of the real Renaissance with all its violence and vitality over the secondhand Renaissance Lucy is holding in the form of photographs of Italian masterpieces. Death teaches them both the value of life and George throws the bloodstained photographs into the river. Her judgment of others begins to change: Miss Lavish and Mr. Eager are "tried by some new test and . . . found wanting" (p. 62). The suburban attitudes of Windy Corner melt under the Italian sun "where anyone who chooses may warm himself in equality" (p. 127). On an outing to Fiesole, in a natural setting typical of Forster settings for significant moments, George kisses Lucy. Her life is opened to the view, although he has to kiss her again after her return home to remind her of it.

George, the right suitor, is the man of action and leaves most of the talking to his father. He is a socialist and a seeker after answers; like his father, he is not given to false chivalry: "his thought, like his behaviour, would not be modified by awe" (p. 52). He experiences life directly and demonstrates this by stealing kisses and leaping into swimming holes.

Forster gives George's actions a spiritual significance by describing them in high style, elevating them to the level of what Forster himself calls prophecy. These are Forster's final words on the swimming episode: "it had been a call to the blood and to the relaxed will, a passing benediction whose influence did not pass, a holiness, a spell, a momentary chalice for youth" (p. 153). George is also frequently associated with Greek gods.[16] One of the problems of the novel is the question of whether George as a character can sustain such associations. It may be an advantage that the right suitor is not didactic, but has this gain not left George merely a relection of his father? Stone calls him his father's "melancholy parrot."[17] Moreover, even if we can forgive George for being his father's echo, should we forgive him for turning Lucy into an echo of himself?

Lucy runs from Florence, lying to herself about her reasons and, upon her return to England, attempts to settle for the unreal, the pretended, in the form of Cecil Vyse, the wrong suitor. Cecil is medieval: "well educated, well endowed, and not deficient physically, he remained in the grip of a certain devil whom the modern world knows as self-consciousness, and whom the medieval, with dimmer vision, worshipped as asceticism" (p. 100). This is the devil Lucy herself has and which she must escape. Described as "well connected" (p. 97), Cecil, ironically, cannot connect with anyone. Lucy sees him rightly as a room without a view, imprisoned in himself. His view of women is possessive and Victorian: "she knew in her heart that she could not trust him, for he desired her untouched" (p. 169); she therefore lies to him about the Emersons who have touched her. Cecil's inability to connect marks him clearly as the wrong suitor for all those who are familiar with Forster's high esteem for "connection"; "only connect" is the epigraph to *Howards End*.

Lucy's engagement to Cecil cannot last because she has learned the value of independence; she has become "a rebel who desired, not a wider dwelling-room, but equality beside the man she loved" (p. 128). Although Forster easily, and over hastily perhaps, rejects financial independence for Lucy—she is not to be allowed to "mess with typewriters and latch-keys"

(p. 226)—it is undoubtedly in the name of a firsthand life, of being her own person, that Cecil, with all his inherited views, is rejected.

However, Lucy has learned her new values from George. George has told her what to think of Cecil. He is not meant for intimacy: "He is the sort who are all right so long as they keep to things—books, pictures—but kill when they come to people.... Every moment of his life he's forming you, telling you what's charming or amusing or ladylike, telling you what a man thinks womanly; and you, you of all women, listen to his voice instead of your own" (p. 194). When Lucy rejects Cecil, she argues for her right "to face the truth" instead of getting it secondhand through him, but she uses George's words to reject him: "You were all right as long as you kept to things, but when you came to people" (p. 202). Even Cecil senses that "a new person seems speaking through you" (p. 202). Perhaps Forster means this scene to be ironic but, if so, the irony is misplaced. Lucy has become George, not herself, and in so doing has undercut Forster's stated view of female maturity. The two suitors convention has confused the novel's statement.

The final chapter is entitled "The End of the Middle Ages"; here we are obviously meant to see Lucy as mature, but she is behaving as much like a "little woman" as any Dickens heroine. She sits with George in their honeymoon room in Florence, darning his socks, allowing him to behave like a baby, finding it endearing that he is sometimes wrong but protecting his male ego from the truth by never telling him when he is. Is this the great comradeship of equals?

Ann Veronica is the first novel in which H.G. Wells deliberately undertook to write about a social problem and thus began those novels of ideas which were to draw so much criticism from his friend Henry James. Although there is nothing in *Ann Veronica* which a modern reader would consider sexually explicit, in its openness about sexual relationships and the opposition it evoked, the novel foreshadowed the later battles over James Joyce and D.H. Lawrence. As in the case of Dreiser's *Sister Carrie*, the objection was not so much that Ann Veronica has an affair with a married man but that her creator approves this and does not subject his heroine to capital punishment for her sin. Reviewers attempted to blame this on what they considered the degeneracy of Wells's own life but, though Wells himself says Ann Veronica is drawn from life, the original model for her creation is not really important to this discussion.

What is more important is Well's reply to a review in the *Spectator*,November 20, 1909, by Joe St. Loe Strachey, the editor, who called the novel a "poisonous book" and claimed that it glorified lust and disregarded self-restraint and "a woman's honour." In his reply Wells defended himself against these charges by defining his aims in writing the novel:

> My book was written primarily to express the resentment and distress which many women feel nowadays at their unavoidable practical dependence upon some individual man not of their deliberate choice, and in full sympathy with the natural but perhaps anarchistic and anti-social idea that it is intolerable for a woman to have sexual relations with a man with whom she is not in love, and natural and desirable and admirable for her to want them, and still more so to want children by a man of her own selection.[18]

In this defense Wells clearly emphasizes the value of a woman's choosing her own mate; it is a biological argument for the importance of natural selection. The goal for a woman, Wells appears to argue, is the freedom to choose one's lover.

The novel itself, however, raises questions of wider and different implications than this. Ann Veronica is supposedly maturing as the novel progresses; she is obviously thinking, fighting for what she wants, and, Wells asks us to believe, developing in the process. But maturity cannot consist merely in the right to choose; it is, in the end, society which gives or denies us this right.

Ann's development is shown in terms of the two suitors convention. The novel Wells claims he has written with its emphasis on natural selection may not conflict with the convention but the novel he has written about female maturity does. A reviewer, R.A. Scott-James, in the *Daily News*, October 4, 1909, recognized that there is a basic problem with the novel's conclusion. He accused Wells of "substituting for the old traditional morality a new morality which is merely its opposite." "Again and again," Scott-James claims, Wells "seemed about to come to quite a different conclusion, to be on the verge of some supreme assertion which would suggest a way of escape for the more sincere theorists of to-day."

Scott-James does not, of course, discuss the structural problem created by the use of the two suitors convention, but he does identify one of the contributing difficulties: Ann Veronica's initial impulse towards rebellion seems to promise a more profound discussion of the complex problems it raises and a less superficial solution to them. What Ann Veronica Stanley must reject is suburbia, which apparently has the same implications for Wells that it does for Forster. She lives with her father and aunt in a London suburb, has had some education at Tredgold Women's College, but sees this as a poor substitute for an Oxford or Cambridge education which her father denied her because "he thought that sort of thing unsexed a woman."[19] She now wishes to go on to further scientific studies at Imperial College. She is described by Wells as "wildly discontented and eager for freedom and life" (p. 3). Her world seems to be "in wrappers, like a house when people leave it for the summer" (p. 4). Ann Veronica "wanted to live ... to do, to be, to experience. . . . She wanted to know" (p. 4). Ann Veronica is, at this stage, a more self-conscious Lucy Honeychurch; the values Wells is advocating for a woman here are those Forster advocates in *A Room with a View:* individuality, being a person in one's own right, experiencing at first hand.

The main stumbling block for Ann Veronica is her father, who epitomizes the Victorian male's attitude to women. He views daughters as possessions: "ownership seemed only a reasonable return for the cares and expenses of a daughter's upbringing" (p. 10). He believes there are "in the matter of age just two feminine classes and no more, girls and women. The distinction lay chiefly in the right to pat their heads" (p. 17).

He is shocked by Ann Veronica's conversation with Mr. Ramage about a play she has seen, about her attendance, hatless, at socialist meetings, about her "disposition to carry her scientific ambitions to unwomanly lengths" (p. 11). In restraining her he thinks he is guided by her best interests; she thinks he is unwilling to let her exist.

Ann Veronica recognizes that the only socially acceptable escape from home is marriage, a route her two sisters have chosen with less than ideal results. She has, therefore, come to see married people as "insects that have lost their wings" (p. 58). She envies her brothers their chance to stand on their own feet and feels "acutely the desire for free initiative, for a life unhampered by others" (p. 58). She tells Mr. Ramage, a middle-aged acquaintance of her father's who is apparently sympathetic to her impulse for freedom, that she wants independence: "It's just to feel—one owns oneself" (p. 63), she explains. Gradually, Ann Veronica comes to see that she is not "just up against Morningside Park and father, but . . . the whole order of things" (p. 182). She sees that "a woman's life is all chance. It's artificially chance. Find your man, that's the rule . . . He will let you live if it pleases him"(p. 183). Ann Veronica comes to find woman's dependence on man as a monstrous limitation, describes woman's life as a "pit" (p. 178). Her frustation and her outrage are convincing and sympathetic; Wells appears to approve them.

The wrong suitor in this novel is really two wrong suitors, Mr. Ramage and Mr. Manning, each of whom represents half of the whore-madonna view of women. Ann Veronica initially runs to London after rejecting a marriage proposal from Mr. Manning, who offers her a life in Morningside Park just like the one she wishes to escape. Mr. Manning treats women as madonnas—"so serene, so fine, so feminine . . . I am a woman worshipper" (p. 40)—but as madonnas who can be owned. They are, after all, "parasites and toys" (p. 34). Like Cecil Vyse and Willoughby Patterne, Hubert Manning believes "the man's share in life [is] to shield, to protect, to lead and toil and watch and battle with the world at large" (p. 44). His imagery, like Cecil's, is medieval: he wants to be her knight and talks of keeping her shut in what Ann Veronica suggests is a "sort of beautiful garden close" (p. 104). Her reasons for rejecting Manning are clearly spelled out in a letter she writes to him; she is fighting for her own identity: "I want to be a person by myself, and to pull my own strings. I had rather have trouble and hardship like that than be taken care of by others. I want to be myself" (p. 86).

In London Ann Veronica finds it impossible to obtain suitable employment and is driven to borrow money from Mr. Ramage who, she believes, genuinely supports her efforts. All Mr. Ramage believes is that he is supporting Ann Veronica and that this entitles him to certain privileges in exchange. His view of women is as reactionary as Mr. Manning's and less flattering: "You women, with your tricks of evasion, you're a sex of swindlers. You have all the instinctive dexterity of parasites" (p.170). This is, of course, simply the other side of Mr. Manning's coin; both believe that "Men do services for the love of women, and the woman who takes must pay" (p.171). After Ramage attempts to seduce her, Ann Veronica sees that both men must be rejected, though in a moment of panic she does temporarily engage herself to Mr. Manning. She begins to recognize the difficulty of escaping dependence on men: "For the first time, it seemed to her, she faced the facts of a woman's position in the world—the meagre realities of such freedom as it permitted her, the almost unavoidable obligation to some individual man under which she must labour for even a foothold in the world" (p.174).

Ann Veronica's brief involvement with the emancipators of the time offers no solution either. It is at this point, I think, that Wells begins to muddle his argument. The chief representative of the feminist movement is Miss Miniver, an easy target for Wells. Absurd, unattractive and muddleheaded— "the Higher Thought, the Simple Life, Socialism, Humanitarianism, it was all the same really" (p.109)—Miss Miniver is finally exposed as merely a woman who is afraid of sex: "'Bodies! Bodies! Horrible things! We are souls!'" (p.144). Wells has adopted the favorite male retort to feminism, reducing it to lack of feminine attractiveness, fear and frigidity. Ann Veronica, quite rightly, sees that Miss Miniver represents no image to emulate but, quite wrongly, takes her, as Wells does, to be typical of all feminists.

Ann Veronica turns instead to her scientific work under Russell and his assistant Capes at Imperial College. She values this because it is relevant: "it made every other atmosphere she knew seem discursive and confused" (p.133). It teaches Ann Veronica a method to apply to all the questions of life: "it was, after all, a more systematic and particular method of examining just the same questions that underlay the discussions of the Fabian Society, the talk of the West Central Arts Club, the chatter of the studios, and the deep, the bottomless discussions of the simplelife homes" (p.134). It is clear enough that Wells will use this to argue the biological imperative he plans to make the solution to Ann Veronica's problems, but he has placed himself in a trap. He is arguing for the ruthless investigation of all questions, logically and rationally, but he avoids the implications he himself has raised in the novel.

Having argued strongly for the necessity for female independence, having given Ann Veronica a sympathetic desire for her own identity, he then allows her to retreat from this position when she falls in love with Capes. In falling back on the old argument that a woman only needs the right man to make her forget all the foolishness about independence, Wells does not allow for a world in which Ann Veronica can be physically attracted to Capes without surrendering her identity to his. True to the convention of the two suitors, Capes is already the representative of scientific truth, of bodily honesty, of unconventional sexual behavior; he is her biology teacher and, although married, has already had an affair before Ann Veronica meets him. Ann merely learns his values, becomes Capes. Ann Veronica is not so far from Jane Austen's world as she believes when she runs off with Capes to the Alps in the footsteps of Vernon Whitfield and Clara Middleton.

Wells appears to recognize the implications of his structure, for he changes the argument to suit it. We are asked to believe that Ann Veronica comes to realize that a woman is naturally subservient: a woman "wants to be free—she wants to be

legally and economically free, so as not to be subject to the
wrong man; but only God, who made the world, can alter
things to prevent her being slave to the right one" (p. 206). No
pretense here at the comradeship of equals, though Capes has
used the phrase earlier. Ann Veronica completely accepts
inferiority: "I'm a female thing at bottom. I like high tone for a
flourish and stars and ideas; but I want my things" (p. 271). In
the final scene, Wells rightly reconciles a pregnant Ann
Veronica and Capes, now married to each other, with her
family in Morningside Park. They are about to be reabsorbed
into suburbia, but it is, surely, Wells rather than God who is
responsible.

Although Gissing's *The Odd Women* was written earlier
than either *A Room with a View* or *Ann Veronica*, it nevertheless seems much more modern in its treatment of the woman
question; indeed, some of Gissing's insights into the psychol-
ogy of the relationship between men and women would not
disgrace a contemporary feminist. The woman question was
exactly that, a question, for Gissing; he made it central to four
of his novels, *The Emancipated* (1890), *The Odd Women*
(1892), *In the Year of the Jubilee* (1894), *The Whirlpool* (1897),
and introduced it into all subsequent ones.

Gissing's letters and novels reveal a strong sympathy with
the idea of female emancipation and he argues it on the same
grounds as the modern women's movement: liberation for
women will bring about true liberation for men. His favorite
novelists were women: George Eliot, Charlotte Brontë, George
Sand; he agreed with the views John Stuart Mill had expressed in *The Subjection of Women*; he believed that women are
the spiritual and mental equals of men and that their subjection in a position of inferiority is responsible for the misery of
both men and women in marriage. In the novels, Gissing
argues, as do Meredith, Forster, and Wells, for the marriage of
comrades.

In *The Odd Women*, Gissing is concerned with the situation
of women in society, particularly with lack of financial
independence which forces them either to marry for security,
as one heroine of the novel, Monica Madden, marries Edmund
Widdowson, or be reduced to an impoverished spinsterhood

because their lack of training prevents their employment. Rhoda Nunn, the other heroine of the novel, wants to give women this training. She helps a friend, Mary Barfoot, run a secretarial school for middle-class girls who are unlikely to marry. Rhoda calls the girls "the odd women," whom society calls useless and whom she sees as "a great reserve."[20]

Mary Barfoot has founded her school on the conviction that women can do everything men can do, except those jobs demanding physical strength. Mary Barfoot and Rhoda Nunn intend girls "to be brought up to a calling in life, just as men are" (p. 98). It is, however, important to recognize that Gissing's point goes much beyond the question of financial independence for unmarried women; he is concerned with all women and with their right and need to function as independent agents. Mary Barfoot's speech entitled "Woman as Invader" makes Gissing's attitude clear; she is obviously intended as his spokesman: "I am not chiefly anxious that you should *earn money*, but that women in general shall become *rational and responsible human beings*" (p. 135).

The story of Monica Madden, like that of Ann Veronica, looks forward, in part, to that version of the two suitors convention we find in the contemporary fiction of such novelists as Doris Lessing and Joyce Carol Oates: the husband had become the wrong suitor who represents a restricted bourgeois life; the other suitor is now the lover who represents freedom. I have deliberately avoided using the term "right suitor," although it is certainly applicable to contemporary fiction where both author and heroine are usually on the side of the lover, because Gissing does not support either husband or lover as right suitor.

Monica Madden is one of five sisters, two of whom soon die, in an overprotected middle-class family. Mr. Madden, like Mr. Stanley, holds firmly to a traditional view of women. His daughters will never "have to distress themselves about money matters" (p. 1). They receive an education "suitable to their breeding" (p. 2), that is one which is totally impractical: "For, as to training them for any path save those trodden by English ladies of the familiar type, he could not have dreamt of any such thing" (p. 3). Mr. Madden does not, of course, expect to die suddenly in an accident before he has made provision for his family, but his expectations are frustrated and he leaves Virginia and Alice "already grown up into uselessness" and Monica to become "half a lady and half a shop-girl" (p. 107).

Virginia and Alice are bad examples for Monica. Huddled together in a small room, they count their tiny private income and make vague plans for opening a school. They have been taught to be passive and cannot take the initiative in any-thing. Virginia finds some relief in alcohol. Monica, who at first appears to be the typical naive heroine with little individuality of character, is considered pretty and therefore likely to escape her sisters' life through marriage. Meanwhile, she works wretchedly in a shop believing that her only hope is to be rescued by a man. For this reason, when she meets Edmund Widdowson, a middle-aged man of independent means, on her Sunday outing, she encourages his attentions even though she has not met him under socially acceptable circumstances and has no feeling for him personally. He represents security and she agrees to marry him in spite of the fact that he is old, has a "stiff dry way," and has already begun "to show how precise and exacting he could be" (p. 68). Her flatmate, Mildred, warns Monica: "you will marry him for a comfortable home—that's what it amounts to. And you'll repent it bitterly some day—you'll repent" (p. 111).

Widdowson has the traditional view of marriage. A woman is a toy to him—he calls Monica a butterfly—and he has no sense that "a wife remains an individual, with rights and obligations independent of her wifely condition" (p. 152). He tells Monica that women belong at home and suggests that she read John Ruskin whose every word about women he believes "good and precious" (p. 153). Although he has little religious faith himself, he views "religion as a precious and powerful instrument for directing the female conscience" (p. 154). Widdowson jealously guards Monica at home, trying for a long time to forbid any outside social visits for her. This male attitude to women appears frequently in fiction—we have already seen it in Willoughby Patterne, Hubert Manning, and Cecil Vyse—but Gissing does more than define it. He reveals the psychological motive for its existence. When Widdowson rejects Monica's request to be taken on a trip abroad, Gissing comments, "Above everything he dreaded humiliation in Monica's sight; it would be intolerable to have her comparing him with men who spoke foreign languages and were at home on the continent" (p. 158).

Monica only knows that she feels trapped and wants freedom. She cannot accept Widdowson's view that housework is a privilege as well as a duty and talks vaguely of making more friends and of reading different kinds of books. She argues that there is not "much real difference between men and women" (p. 163) but Widdowson finds that to "regard her simply as a human being was beyond the reach of his intelligence" (p. 237). Mary Barfoot and Rhoda Nunn have already shown Monica the road to independence and self-respect before her marriage, but she was unable to recognize it then and cannot now. Just as security had to be found in a man, so does freedom. Freedom to Monica is necessarily sexual freedom; it is all she can envision. Her imagination is as limited as her husband's.

When she meets an attractive young man, Mr. Bevis, who flirts with her, he rapidly comes to represent the freedom she desires. He sets up a meeting alone with her and offers to take her abroad with him. Traditional as ever, Monica believes that all she has ever wanted is "freedom to love." Bevis is the man "who should have been her husband. Him she could love with heart and soul, could make his will her absolute law, could live on his smiles, could devote herself to his interests" (p. 222). Wells ends *Ann Veronica* on this note, but Gissing understands the falseness of it. Monica has not understood the nature of flirtation. When Bevis is taken seriously, he reveals his cowardly nature and abandons Monica. Widdowson finds out about her flirtation, though he suspects Everard Barfoot and not Bevis, and, even though Monica is pregnant with his child, cannot forgive her.

Gissing offers neither Widdowson nor Bevis, who in many contemporary novels would have represented freedom, as the right suitor. He clearly sees that Bevis represents only an illusory freedom; freedom cannot be found in another human being. Nevertheless in spite of this insight, Gissing clings to some of the trappings of the convention. Monica dies and is thus punished for her sin in typical nineteenth-century fashion; in fact her punishment is harsher for her sin consists in nothing more than confessing an attraction to a man over afternoon tea.

The most significant aspect of The Odd Women is the character of Rhoda Nunn, an old friend of the Madden family, who at fifteen finds "her sole pleasure . . . in intellectual talk" (p. 3). She gives herself a practical education—shorthand, book-keeping, commercial correspondance, typewriting—regretting her lack of piano lessons only because they would have made her fingers more supple for typing. When Virginia Madden renews acquaintance with her, Rhoda is working at Mary Barfoot's school and inspires Virginia with "strange new thoughts . . . . It was the first time in her life that she had spoken with a woman daring enough to think and act for herself" (p. 24). Like Wilkie Collins's Marian Halcombe and Charlotte Brontë's Shirley Keeldar, Rhoda is, of course, described as "masculine," with "an expression somewhat aggressive" (p. 20), "quite like a man in energy and resources" (p. 30); even Gissing cannot escape stereotyping. Rhoda differs from Mary Barfoot in believing an independent working life superior to marriage for a woman, maintaining "the vast majority of women lead a vain and miserable life because they do marry" (p. 59). She wishes to teach girls that given the present attitude of men and society, "for the majority of women marriage means disgrace" (p. 99), since marriage will not allow them to be complete human beings. She does, however, allow for the possibility of a future world in which women "are trained to self-respect . . . and marriage may be honourable to both" (pp. 99-100).

Independence is one choice for Rhoda, a choice she has already made when the novel opens but which still worries her a little. Has she merely chosen independence because no man has proposed to her? Would she still choose it if she fell in love with a man who wanted her? The test comes through Everard Barfoot, Mary's cousin, an impudent, witty, intelligent man who entertains Rhoda when they first meet with stories of his friends' unhappy marriages. "Why will men marry fools?" Rhoda asks him and finds that Everard shares her views on the necessity of educating women. "In my mind," Everard tells her, "you are working for the happiness of men" (p. 102).

At first Rhoda represents a challenge for Everard. How flattering it would be to make this woman fall in love with him! "Had she a vein of sentiment in her character?" (p. 126). But he does not allow for falling in love with her himself. Gradually he comes to recognize that "a man might do worse than secure her for his comrade through the whole journey of life" (p. 130). Deciding to reject him, Rhoda is nevertheless attracted by the notion of triumph, that she could raise her finger "and Everard Barfoot would marry her" (p. 186). But, like Everard, she has not allowed for falling in love and, meeting him on a walking tour, she realizes that she loves "with passion" (p. 264). They agree initially on an open relationship without marriage.

Doubts, however, set in before this relationship begins and both fall back into traditional attitudes. Like Monica, they cannot escape their conditioning, a conditioning to which Gissing sees novelists as major contributors: "If every novelist could be strangled and thrown into the sea we should have some chance of reforming women" (p. 58). Contemplating a future with Everard, Rhoda finds she needs a legal bond. When she hears the false rumors about Monica Madden's affair with Everard, she becomes conventionally jealous. Everard, meanwhile, has been flirting, conventionally, with all the attractive female objects he meets. Rhoda recognizes that marriage is impossible. Passion means more to her now: "Her conception of life was larger, more liberal; she made no vows to crush the natural instincts," but she knows she must remain "the same proud and independent woman" (p. 291). The novel ends with Rhoda's return to her independent life and her planning the education of Monica's infant daughter. It is an honest but bleak conclusion as Rhoda contemplates the little girl's struggles with the world and murmurs "Poor little child!" (p. 336).

In The Odd Women, Gissing has perhaps come closer than

any other nineteenth-century novelist both to foreshadowing the new form the two suitors convention will take in the twentieth century and to suggesting a direction future novelists might more profitably take in portraying the maturing of a central female characer. In the story of Monica Madden he has foreshadowed the form of the convention in which the right suitor is a lover who shows the way to freedom. In the story of Rhoda Nunn Gissing has managed to show a woman grow to maturity without defining this growth entirely through her relationships with men. Rhoda's qualities are her own, not the reflection of those of any male character in the novel. Rhoda works, relates to her colleague and partner, worries about the problems connected with that work, and also falls in love. Gissing has shown the road forward but, surprisingly, it is a road few twentieth-century novelists have chosen to follow.

Conclusion

ONE REASON that no novelist pursued the path Gissing indicated is, as I suggested in my introduction, that the early twentieth century saw some dramatic changes in the subject matter and techniques of fiction. The most interesting British novelists of this period—with the exception of D.H. Lawrence—did not write the kind of apprenticeship novel I have been discussing. Reality no longer seemed so fixed, so ascertainable, so maturity could hardly lie in perceiving it. The subjectivity of the individual vision was to many the only certainty, and the dramatization of this required techniques which would convey the activity of the mind itself. The novels of Virginia Woolf, then, provide no solution to the structural problems raised by the novels of Charlotte Brontë or of George Eliot because they aim to do something quite different. Lily Briscoe, for example, may develop during the action of *To the Lighthouse,* but her growth is not the kind of societal maturing which Dorothea Brooke and Lucy Honeychurch undergo.

Now, in the seventies, the situation of women in society is once again a topic of major concern, and novels dealing with the maturing of a central female character are appearing, in both England and the U.S.A., with a frequency unknown since the nineteenth century. With the renewal of this interest has come a rebirth of the two suitors convention, updated, of course, in modern dress, but the same convention nonetheless. The formula of the contemporary version of the two suitors convention is basically that of a much earlier novel, D.H. Lawrence's *Lady Chatterley's Lover* (1928): a woman leaves her husband, who, as the representative of the dead, traditional life, is the wrong suitor, and takes a lover, the embodiment of freedom and of sexual-spiritual rebirth, and therefore the right suitor. It is the formula suggested in an 1899 American novel, Kate Chopin's *The Awakening*, now enjoying a revival of popularity precisely because it is so like a novel of the nineteen seventies.

If Forster had commented on *A Room With A View* seventy years later instead of fifty,[1] his version of the Lucy and George story would have gone something like this. Lucy and George have been married twenty years—the contemporary version of the convention always begins after marriage—and live in a London suburb. Lucy is bored; giving music lessons is not sufficiently fulfilling and the children are demanding. She feels that George takes her for granted, that she has no individual identity but is merely his wife. She experiences a sort of schizophrenia as the "real" Lucy reasserts herself. Enter Cecil Vyse, now the right suitor—debonair, cosmopolitan, the representative of a wider, freer life. Lucy leaves George for an affair with Cecil through which she hopes to find herself. This adaption of the two suitors convention has the same problems as the original. A definition of maturity as individuality and the freedom to express it inevitably conflicts with the structural implications of the two suitors convention. Lucy cannot find herself simply by following Cecil.

In spite of greater consciousness of the situation of women, a great number of contemporary novelists seem as trapped in the two suitors convention as their ancestors. In the early years of the seventies, the bored housewife novel became a subgenre of its own, so much so that, when Brian Moore's *The Doctor's Wife* appeared in 1976, it seemed strangely outdated, despite its open ending. The story of the middle-class wife who seeks liberation through a love affair with a younger man in Europe had surely been told before. It strongly resembled, for example, Doris Lessing's *The Summer Before the Dark*, and had similarities to Erica Jong's *Fear of Flying*. These novels, both published in 1973, clearly illustrate the problems with the contemporary version of the two suitors convention. It is surely a further indication of the persistence of the convention that it limits even novelists who have helped to change contemporary consciousness about women and might reasonably be expected to find new fictional structures to express their insights.

Doris Lessing's *The Summer Before the Dark* reflects an awareness of the problems with the convention but provides no solution to them. The first half of the novel is similar in structure to Oates's *Do With Me What You Will*, although the heroines are very different. Kate Brown, forty-five years old, has been married to Michael Brown for twenty-five years. She is fully aware of her own dissatisfactions and what they mean. She lacks choice; she is forced to fit herself to certain roles—suburban housewife, mother; she describes herself as "a doormat," "a cripple." One summer, looking back on her life, she decides she has acquired not virtues but a form of dementia.

In an attempt to find the "real" Kate, she takes a job which does not provide the answer. The real Kate, symbolically represented in her dreams as a sick seal that must be carried to safety, is still unfulfilled. The job does, however, provide Jeffrey Merton, a thirty-two year old American who is apparently to be the right suitor. He offers Kate a chance of freedom through sexual expression. What is more, Kate finds in Jeffrey a definition of her own choice. He, too, is torn between conventional responsibility and freedom; in his case between a law career in New York and a life of continued wandering in Europe. She chooses an affair with Jeffrey and a vacation in Spain but all she acquires from him is a strange illness which leaves him in Spain and brings Kate back to London.

Lessing is apparently not content to make a young lover the solution to the problems of a forty-five-year-old woman. For a while Kate shares the apartment of a young girl in London. Once again she falls into the role of mother but the girl has no desire to play daughter. If Kate learns anything here, it is not easy to see what it is. Yet at this point Lessing asks us to believe that Kate has grown, has changed. She returns to her old suburban street, thinner, her hair no longer dyed, and the neighbors do not recognize her. The seal in her dream has recovered, a sign, one supposes, of Kate's maturing.

But what has brought about this maturation? Has Jeffrey changed her or not? Lessing's answer is not clear. The ambiguity of Jeffrey's position gives rise to a greater structural difficulty. Lessing may have rejected the contemporary version of the two suitors convention as dishonest, but where is she to go with this novel? She has defined Kate's experience up to this point through her relationships with two men and a girl. But what now? What is Kate to do with this freedom she has supposedly gained? Lessing apparently has no other answer than to return her neatly to husband Michael. Kate and Doris Lessing are, it seems, certain that she will not succumb to the old submissive ways but it is hard to agree with them. It is even harder to accept this supposedly significant spiritual growth as sufficiently expressed in a change of hair style: "She was saying no: no, no, no, no: a statement which would be concentrated in her hair."[2] For all the feminist arguments against dismissing images as trivial because they are associated primarily with women or with women's lives, there is surely some irony involved in expressing Kate's new life through something symbolic of the imprisoning domesticity of the old. *The Summer Before the Dark*, then, is finally a confused statement,[3] confused, in part at least, becuase Lessing has no alternative yet to some form of the two suitors convention.

Erica Jong's *Fear of Flying* is not the better of these novels but it is perhaps the more interesting in terms of my discussion because Jong is so obviously aware of the convention within which she is writing. Isadora Wing, the heroine, starts where Kate Brown does. She is married to Bennett Wing, a Chinese psychiatrist, and is bored. Like Kate Brown, she understands her dissatisfaction and blames it as much on the institution of marriage itself and its failure to fulfill the expectations of a modern American female as upon the specific faults of her husband. Isadora wants to discover if she "is still whole after so many years of being half of something (like the back legs of a horse outfit on the vaudeville stage)."[4]

At a psychiatric convention in Vienna she meets Adrian Goodlove, a tweedy English psychiatrist, and lusts after him. In spite of the frequently noted feminist reversal in this novel which makes the man a sex object, Jong is nevertheless working, structurally, within a very old convention. And she knows it. Adrian, the representative of freedom, is undercut from the beginning. His existentialism, which he defines as never talking about the future, has been learned in a one week's crash course with a French prostitute. He offers Isadora freedom—an unplanned car trip around Europe—but she regresses to adolescence and practices writing her new name on scraps of paper: Mrs. Adrian Goodlove. She leaves Bennett and runs off with Adrian. "What else could I do?" Erica Jong remarks self-consciously through Isadora, "I had painted myself into a corner, I had written myself into this hackneyed plot" (p. 173).

Fear of Flying seems set to become a parody of the contemporary two suitors convention at this moment but, unfortunately, it slips back into a mere illustration of it. Erica Jong has realized the absurdity of being given freedom by the new lover but she has nowhere to go now with her novel. The trip with Adrian is a disaster and so is the plot from this point on. The next several chapters consist of Isadora's description of her earlier relationships with men. The book degenerates into a series of short stories, none of them essential to the plot or a significant comment on the present action.

Finally, after Adrian has left—the man with the unplanned future turns out to have an unbreakable commitment to meet his exwife for a vacation—Isadora returns to the hotel in London where she believes her husband is staying. She goes to his room to wait for him. This is *The Summer Before the Dark* once again; but Erica Jong struggles overtly with the structural problem. She even entitles this chapter "A 19th-Century Ending." She tries to suggest the ending is open but knows it is not. Isadora says, "It was not clear how it would end. In nineteenth-century novels, they get married. In twentieth-century novels they get divorced. Can you have an ending in which they do neither? I laughed at myself for being so literary. 'Life has no plot' is one of my favorite lines" (p. 311).

Novels of course do have plots and, when the heroine's development has been described entirely in terms of "them," then the ending requires that "they" do something. As Isadora is washing her hair, Bennett walks in. The two suitors convention has forced an ending. Erica Jong's awareness of the falsity of the seventies adaptation, which would have left Isadora with Adrian, has only driven her back to the nineteenth-century version.

What are the problems for such novelists as Lessing and Jong? Is it possible that they really believe women's lives are defined entirely through their relationships to men? That seems unlikely. Their own existence as writers surely denies the implications of their novels' structures. "Why," asks Norma Rosen in a 1974 New York Times article, has no contemporary female novelist "created a character whose inner life approached anything like the scope or the range of possibility of the creator's own?"[5]

Is it, then, that they cannot yet see other possibilities for the novel, that they are indeed victims of literary convention? This seems more probable, and is supported by the fact that the female poets of the seventies have developed new styles while the novelists on the whole have not. This could simply not have been the case if the problem was sociological rather than literary.

Adrienne Rich's article,"When We Dead Awaken,"[6] discusses her artistic development from the point when she realized that her style had been created by the formalism of such modern male poets as Auden, Stevens, MacNeice to her acceptance of the need to describe her own experiences directly. The identifiable style of the new feminist poets has involved, as Rich says, a breaking with the formalism of modern poetry which demanded a nonfemale universality.

The novelists, however, have faced different problems. In spite of the modern experiments of such novelists as Joyce, the novel has always sustained some sort of realistic tradition, has seen its basic function as more closely related to social experience. For this reason, with the renewed interest in a social issue which fiction seems admirably suited to discuss, it is understandable that contemporary novelists should return to the forms of an earlier strong tradition of realistic fiction. It seems more probable that Doris Lessing has been influenced by George Eliot, for example, than that Adrienne Rich should be affected by Elizabeth Barrett Browning.

Only gradually, though, are contemporary female novelists becoming aware that in returning to a nineteenth-century concern, they have also revived a nineteenth-century convention. The two suitors convention may have been established and sustained to a large extent by women writers but it is, of course, patriarchal in nature. Its structure implies the inferiority and necessary subordination of women. The women who used it, even while struggling to express feminist views within it, were writing for male judges and often under assumed male names.

There are some indications that women novelists are looking in new directions; the contemporary heroine is occasionally shown now in relationships which are not primarily sexual. The publication of Adrienne Rich's *Of Woman Born* (1976), a study of motherhood as experience and institution, was extremely timely. Increasingly, women are becoming aware that acquiring a strong female identity may mean recognizing one's relationship to a matriarchal tradition. On the simplest level, this is reflected in fiction as the investigation of the heroine's relationship to her mother. Rosellen Brown's *The Autobiography of My Mother* (1976) takes this as its chief subject and the best section of Margaret Atwood's *Lady Oracle* (1976) is probably the comically treated but very perceptive analysis of the motivations of the heroine's mother. In Margaret Laurence's *The Diviners* (1974) Morag Gunn, a writer living alone apart from occasional visits from her daughter Pique, comes to terms with her own life through establishing her connection to her past and sees her daughter beginning the same process with her.

More fundamentally, the emphasis on the mother becomes an interest in older matriarchal traditions which are often used to investigate the whole question of what it means to be female. The mythic quality of Lois Gould's *A Sea Change* (1976) arises from its concern with this subject; Gail Pass's upcoming *Surviving Sisters* defines its heroine's development in part through her relationship to the ancient matriarchal religions. An important matriarchal strain in Margaret Atwood's *Surfacing* (1972) has been largely overlooked by critics. Using the familiar formula of a child's search for the father, Atwood's female protagonist finally encounters a monstrous image of what he has become which, she says, has nothing to tell her after all. She also sees the ghost of her mother, standing quietly, surrounded by birds, her hand stretched out. Her mother recognizes that she is there and then disappears into nature again as one of the birds. The heroine learns that female strength resides in what is nonviolent, natural, and nourishing.

Increasing numbers of novels explore women's relationships with other women, some, but not all, of which are lesbian. Virginia Woolf said in *A Room of One's Own* that to read the words "Chloe liked Olivia" in a novel was very strange to her. "I tried to remember," she writes, "any case in the course of my reading where two women are represented as friends. . . . There are now and then mothers and daughters. But almost without exception they are shown in their relationship to men."[7] Nowadays she would still be surprised but perhaps not quite so strongly. Such novels as Rita Mae Brown's *Rubyfruit Jungle* (1973), Marge Piercy's *Small-Changes* (1972), Isabel Miller's *Patience and Sarah* (1969), May Sarton's *Mrs. Stevens Hears the Mermaids Singing* (1965), and Gail Pass's *Zoe's Book* (1976) have made women's relationships with each other a viable subject for fiction. There is a danger, of course, in merely substituting another woman for the right suitor, a danger which Marge Piercy and Isabel Miller do not entirely escape. More often, though, these novelists allow their heroines independent development. As Elizabeth Fishel says, the awakenings of feminist heroines "occur not *because* of personal relationships, but *in spite of* them, or rather, in the intricate process of self-definition that occurs willy-nilly in the midst of them."[8] Rita Mae Brown's heroine is defined as much through the film she makes as through her female lovers, and Gail Pass's *Zoe's Book* assumes the validity of lesbian relationships in the course of discussing its true subject, the nature of the fictional experience.

There are fewer novels in which a heroine's heterosexual relationships are balanced with her relationship to her work and in most of these the work is, understandably, either academic or literary. Perhaps the most interesting example to date is Gail Godwin's *The Odd Woman* (1974) which is as concerned with its heroine's experiences as a college teacher as with her affair with her married lover. Indeed, Godwin takes as her subject the relationship between between love and personal independence. Obviously recognizing the significance of the path Gissing opened up in 1898, she adapts his title and uses allusions to *The Odd Women* throughout her novel.

Although heroines are gradually being shown in other relationships, this in itself does not provide an alternative fictional structure to the two suitors convention. The formula by which a woman is compared to two men and eventually paired with one of them may be disappearing, but there is little sign yet of viable new structures. For all its concern with matriarchal traditions, the possibility of literal new birth at the end of *Surfacing* raises too many problems to be truly satisfying. Are we far enough away from the idea of motherhood as a restriction on independence and as the only possible function of a woman to accept the notion of giving birth as a positive statement about a protagonists's maturity? There are endings which are essentially literary and thus avoid a major difficulty, but these are necessarily of limited application. After all, only when the heroine is a writer, as in *The Diviners* and Lessing's *The Golden Notebook,* can the novel conclude with our realization that she is writing it. The structure of these new feminist novels is more frequently loosely episodic culminating in an open ending. The conclusion of *The Odd Woman* is typical: Jane Clifford has left her lover and is granted an extension, a short one, of her academic contract. Nothing is sure about her future, but almost anything is possible.

Of course it is true that most contemporary novels with male protagonists have similar patterns and similar endings. Some awareness of individual identity is established, some accomodation to the situation is made, but there is no very clear sense of future direction. The difficulty in establishing viable fictional structures apparently affects all contemporary novelists whether their protagonists are male or female. What we should perhaps recognize is that the heroine is now in this respect the equal of the hero, albeit a contemporary hero and therefore, like her, frustrated and uncertain.

Notes

Introduction

1. Patricia Meyer Spacks, *The Female Imagination* (1975; rpt. New York: Avon Books, 1976), p. 4. A failure to make a distinction between social and literary conventions seriously mars most of the reviews of Kate Millett's *Flying*, and, to some extent, Elizabeth Hardwick's *Seduction and Betrayal.*

2. Such comments as Vineta Colby's in *Yesterday's Woman: Domestic Realism in the English Novel* (Princeton: Princeton University Press, 1974), p. 3, are all too rare: "they [the minor novelists] do not account for the creative genius of the major novelists, but they provided themes and ideas, they shaped styles and formed attitudes toward a still new art form."

3. By "feminism as style" I mean both investigations of such questions as what Virginia Woolf means by "the feminine sentence" and examinations of sexist language in such works as Millett's *Sexual Politics* and Annette Kolodny's psycholinguistic study *The Lay of the Land* (Chapel Hill: University of North Carolina Press, 1975).

4. The convention of the two suitors is clear evidence of the novel's origins in drama and it has retained all the artificiality and formality of romantic comedy. See David Cecil, *Hardy the Novelist* (London: Constable and Son, Ltd., 1943), p. 37: "Fielding and his followers took for granted that a more accurate chronicle of ordinary life would be intolerably dull to the reader. So they evolved a working compromise. The setting and characters of their stories were fitted into a framework of non-realistic plot derived from the drama, consisting of an intrigue delivered by all sorts of sensational events—conspiracies, children changed at birth, mistakes of identity—centering round a handsome ideal hero and heroine and a sinister villain, and solved neatly in the last chapter."

5. Marvin Mudrick, *Jane Austen: Irony or Defense and Discovery* (Princeton: Princeton University Press, 1952), p. 40. I do not mean to imply that Jane Austen's values are those of the novel of sensibility. For more detailed discussions of the hero-anti-hero origins of the convention in eighteenth-century fiction see Alexander Welsh, *The Hero of the Waverly Novels* (New Haven: Yale University Press, 1963) and Percy G. Adams, "The Anti-hero in Eighteenth-Century Fiction," *Studies in the Literary Imagination* 9, no. 1 (Spring 1976): 29-52.

6. Spacks, p. 77, makes some interesting comments on marriage as the ending to the Victorian novel.

7. For a detailed discussion of this subject see the following: Patricia Thomson, *The Victorian Heroine: A Changing Ideal, 1837-73* (London: Oxford University Press, 1956); Hazel Mews, *Frail Vessels: Woman's Role in Women's Novels From Fanny Burney to George Eliot* (London: The Athlone Press, 1969); Jenni Calder, *Women and Marriage in Victorian Fiction* (New York: Oxford University Press, 1976).

8. There are several nineteenth-century novels which describe the life of a governess, the best known being Charlotte Brontë's *Jane Eyre* and Thackeray's *Vanity Fair*. The horrors of such a life are better illustrated in Lady Blessington's *The Governess*.

9. John Ruskin, *The Complete Works* (New York: Thomas Y. Crowell and Co., n.d.) 12: 59-60.

10. Ibid., p. 58.

11. Mary Wollstonecraft, *A Vindication of the Rights of Women* (New York: W.W. Norton and Co., Inc., 1967), p. 101.

12. John Stuart Mill, *On the Subjection of Women* (Greenwich, Conn.: Fawcett, 1971), p. 77.

13. Mrs. Craik, *Olive* (London: Chapman and Hall, 1850), pp. 166-67.

14. Calder, pp. 100-102.

15. See, for example, Sue Kaufman's *Diary of a Mad Housewife,* Edna O'Brien's *Girl with the Green Eyes,* Margaret Drabble's *The Needle's Eye,* Joyce Carol Oates's *Do With Me What You Will,* Erica Jong's *Fear of Flying.*

16. George Gissing, *The Odd Women* (New York: Stein and Day, 1968), p. 58.

17. Doris Lessing, *A Proper Marriage* (New York: New American Library, 1970), p. 206.

Chapter One

1. Two books have been completely devoted to her relationship to her predecessors: Frank Bradbrook, *Jane Austen and Her Predecessors* (Cambridge: Cambridge University Press, 1966); Kenneth

L. Moler, *Jane Austen's Art of Allusion* (Lincoln: University of Nebraska Press, 1968). Others have devoted opening chapters to the subject: see, for example, A. Walton Litz, *Jane Austen: A Study of Her Artistic Development* (New York: Oxford University Press, 1965). See also Henrietta ten Harmsel, *Jane Austen: A Study in Fictional Conventions* (The Hague: Mouton, 1964) and William H. Magee, "The Happy Marriage: The Influence of Charlotte Smith on Jane Austen," *Studies in the Novel* 7 (Spring 1975): 120-32.

2. Tony Tanner, Introduction to *Sense and Sensibility* (Baltimore: Penguin Books, 1969).

3. Dorothy Van Ghent, *The English Novel: Form and Function* (New York: Harper and Row, 1953), p. 107. See also Patricia Meyer Spacks, *The Female Imagination*, p. 148.

4. Moler, p. 11.

5. Tanner, p. 33. Stuart Tave's *Words of Jane Austen* (Chicago: University of Chicago Press, 1973) is especially good on the subject of limitations.

6. Litz, for example, claims that the chapters devoted to literary burlesque, 1-2 and 20-25, form detachable units. See also Marvin Mudrick, *Jane Austen: Irony or Defense and Discovery*, p. 39.

7. Mudrick, p. 47.

8. Jane Austen, *Northanger Abbey*, ed. R.W. Chapman (1818; rpt. London: Oxford University Press, 1933), p. 19. All subsequent page references to this novel are to this edition.

9. Moler disagrees with the use of the term *female quixote* to describe Catherine before she meets Isabella and is introduced to Gothic fiction. We are, however, told that she has been brought up on books if not on Gothic novels.

10. Litz, p. 64.

11. Moler, p. 73. He claims that Elinor is not a standard and that her sense must be seen as ironically as Marianne's sensibility.

12. Jane Austen, *Sense and Sensibility*, ed. R.W. Chapman (1811; rpt. London: Oxford University Press, 1933), p. 378. All subsequent page references to the novel are to this edition.

13. Mudrick, p. 93: "Marianne, the life and center of the novel, has been betrayed, and not by Willoughby."

14. Mudrick, p. 88.

15. Litz, p. 100.

16. Moler, p. 75. Cf. Reuben A. Brower, *The Fields of Light: An Experiment in Critical Reading* (New York: Oxford University Press, 1951), p. 165; Samuel Kliger, "Jane Austen's *Pride and Prejudice* in the Eighteenth Century Mode," *University of Toronto Quarterly* 16 (1947): 357-71; Litz, p. 104.

17. Jane Austen, *Pride and Prejudice*, ed. R.W. Chapman (1813; rpt. London: Oxford University Press, 1932), p. 225. All subsequent page references to the novel are to this edition.

18. Mudrick, p. 161.

19. Kingsley Amis, "What became of Jane Austen," *The Spectator*, 4 October 1957, pp. 339-40.

20. Jane Austen, *Emma*, ed. R.W. Chapman (1816; rpt. London: Oxford University Press, 1933), p. 190. All subsequent page references to the novel are to this edition.

21. Quoted by James Edward Austen-Leigh, *Memoirs of His Aunt* (Oxford: Oxford University Press, 1926), p. 157.

22. Mudrick, pp. 184-85.

23. Edmund Wilson, "A Long Talk About Jane Austen," *Classics and Commercials: A Literary Chronicle of the Forties* (New York: Farrar, Straus & Cudahy, Inc., 1950). Mark Kinkead-Weekes's essay "This Old Maid: Jane Austen Replies to Charlotte Brontë and D.H. Lawrence," *Nineteenth-Century Fiction* 30 (December 1975): 399-420, provides an answer to Mudrick and Wilson.

24. Wayne Booth, *The Rhetoric of Fiction* (Chicago: University of Chicago Press, 1961), pp. 245-46.

25. Jane Austen, *Persuasion*, ed. R.W. Chapman (1818; rpt. London: Oxford University Press, 1933), p. 25. All subsequent page references to the novel are to this edition.

26. See, for example, Moler, p. 191.

27. Andrew Wright discusses this more fully in *Jane Austen's Novels: A Study in Structure* (London: Chatto and Windus, 1961), pp. 160-61. See also David M. Monaghan, "The Decline of the Gentry: A Study of Jane Austen's Attitude to Formality in *Persuasion*," *Studies in the Novel* 7 (Spring 1975): 73-87.

Chapter Two

1. Kathleen Tillotson, *Novels of the Eighteen-Forties* (London: Oxford University Press, 1961), p. 204. Cf. Ellen Moers, *Literary Women: The Great Writers* (New York: Doubleday and Co., 1976), pp. 27-30.

2. Elizabeth Gleghorn Gaskell, *Mary Barton* (1848; rpt. New York: Truslove & Comba, n.d.), p. 10. All subsequent page references to this novel are to this edition.

3. Tillotson, p. 211: "He is bigger than the events, even than the clashing social forces which they represent."

4. Margaret Ganz, *Elizabeth Gaskell: The Artist in Conflict* (New York: Twayne Publishers, Inc., 1969), p. 69.

5. George Eliot, *Felix Holt, The Radical* (1866; rpt. Baltimore: Penguin Books, 1972), p. 153. All subsequent page references to the novel are to this edition.

6. David Cecil, *Victorian Novelists: Essays in Revaluation* (Chicago: University of Chicago Press, 1958), p. 228.

7. Bradford A. Booth, Anthony Trollope: Aspects of his Life and Art (Bloomington: Indiana University Press, 1958), p. 47.
8. Anthony Trollope, Dr. Thorne (1858; rpt. Boston: Houghton Mifflin Co., 1959), p. 14. All subsequent page references to the novel are to this edition.
9. Michael Sadleir, Trollope: A Commentary (London: Oxford University Press, 1961), p. 384.
10. Wilkie Collins, The Woman in White (London: Thomas Nelson and Sons, Ltd., n.d.), p. 61. All subsequent page references to the novel are to this edition.

Chapter Three

1. Margaret Lane, "Introduction," Mrs. Gaskell's Ruth (London: J.M. Dent & Sons Ltd., 1967), p. vi. All page references to Ruth are to this edition.
2. Charlotte Brontë and others saw that death as unnecessary. Margaret Ganz, Elizabeth Gaskell, p. 271, quotes Elizabeth Barrett Browning: "Was it quite impossible but that your Ruth should die?" Nancy Miller's "Female Sexuality and Narrative Structure in La Nouvelle Héloise and Les Liaisons dangereuses," Signs: Journal of Women in Culture and Society 1 (Spring 1976): 609-38 is interesting on the relationship between the death of the heroine and her sexuality.
3. Catherine Earnshaw, of course, dies for sanctioned sexual activity, marriage with Edgar Linton, rather than for a slip from virtue.
4. David Cecil, Victorian Novelists, p. 139. Patricia Meyer Spacks reads the novel as a celebration of adolescent rebellion and its intensities, The Female Imagination, pp. 172ff.
5. Emily Brontë, Wuthering Heights (Boston: Houghton Mifflin Co., 1956), p. 49. All page references to the novel are to this edition. The most interesting discussion of the relationship between Heathcliff and Catherine is Q.D. Leavis's "A Fresh Approach to Wuthering Heights" in F.R. & Q.D. Leavis, Lectures in America (New York: Pantheon Books, 1969), pp. 85-138.
6. William E. Buckler, Introduction to Tess of the d'Urbervilles by Thomas Hardy (Boston: Houghton Mifflin Co., 1960), p. xxii.
7. See, for example, Albert J. Guerard, "Introduction," Hardy: A Collection of Critical Essays, Twentieth Century Views (Englewood Cliffs, N.J.: Prentice Hall, 1963), p. 6: "But the unacademic approach of most of the essayists in this volume seems a more useful one—to regard the philosophy either as intrusive and inert, or at best as a

body of speculation aesthetically useful to Hardy in the writing of his novels and poems, but of no great intrinsic interest to the reader of today."

8. Arnold Kettle's observation on this is worth noting. *An Introduction to the English Novel* (New York: Harper and Row, 1968), p. 234.

9. Donald Davidson makes this point in "The Traditional Basis of Thomas Hardy's Fiction," *Still Rebels, Still Yankees and Other Essays* (Baton Rouge: The Louisiana State Press, 1957), rpt. in Albert Guerard, ed., *Hardy: A Collection of Critical Essays*, p. 19.

10. Ibid., p. 22.

11. D.H. Lawrence, "Hardy's 'Predilection d'artiste,'" *Phoenix* (New York: The Viking Press, 1936), rpt. in Guerard, p. 48.

12. Thomas Hardy, *The Return of the Native*, ed. James Gindin, Norton Critical Edition (New York: W.W. Norton and Co., Inc., 1969), p. 4. All page references to the novel are to this edition.

13. Thomas Hardy, Preface, *Tess of the d'Urbervilles*, ed. William E. Buckler (Boston: Houghton Mifflin Co., 1960), p. xxi. All page references to the novel are to this edition.

14. M.W. Steinberg, Introduction to *Tess of the d'Urbervilles* (New York: The Odyssey Press, 1966), p. xx.

15. See, for examples, Buckler, p. xii and D.H. Lawrence, "A Study of Thomas Hardy," *Phoenix*, rpt. in Thomas Hardy, *Tess of the d'Urbervilles*, ed. Scott Elledge, Norton Critical Edition (New York: W.W. Norton, and Co., Inc., 1965), p. 407.

16. David Lodge, *Language of Fiction* (New York: Columbia University Press, 1966), p. 185.

17. Thomas Hardy, Postscript, *Jude the Obscure*, ed. Irving Howe (Boston: Houghton Mifflin Co., 1965), p. 6. All page references to the novel are to this edition.

18. D.H. Lawrence, "Sue Bridehead," *Phoenix*, rpt. Guerard, p. 76. Kate Millett calls Sue "not only the new woman" but "the Frigid Woman as well" (*Sexual Politics* [1970; rpt. New York: Equinox, 1971] p. 130).

19. Lawrence, "Sue Bridehead," pp. 75-76.

20. In Hardy's novels it is, as I have shown, difficult to know which choice is wrong. For example, is the affair with Wildeve wrong or the marriage to Clym?

Chapter Four

1. All critics agree on this. See, for example, Robert Martin, *Charlotte Brontë's Novels: The Accents of Persuasion* (New York: W.W. Norton and Co., Inc., 1968), p. 30.

2. Karl, A Reader's Guide to the Nineteenth Century British Novel (New York: The Noonday Press, 1964), p. 75. Cf. Kathleen Tillotson, Novels of the Eighteen-Forties, p. 261: "The relation of Jane Eyre to the literature of its time is seen more clearly if we include the poetry being read, and written—the poetry of Wordsworth and Byron, Arnold and Clough."

3. David Cecil, Victorian Novelists, pp. 102-103. Recent critics have done much to counter this view. See for example, discussions of Charlotte Brontë's heroines by Ellen Moers, Patricia Meyer Spacks, Kate Millett and Helene Moglen, Charlotte Brontë: The Self Conceived (New York: W.W. Norton and Co., Inc., 1976.

4. Cecil, Victorian Novelists, p. 103.

5. Ibid.

6. Quoted in Tillotson, p. 278.

7. Walter Allen, The English Novel: A Short Critical History, (New York: E.P. Dutton and Co., Inc., 1954), p. 215. Cf. Martin, p. 42: "All her heroines look to their lovers for domination in one form or another."

8. Mary A. Ward, Introduction to Shirley, by Charlotte Brontë (London: Smith, Elder and Co., 1905), p. xxiv. All subsequent page references to this novel are to this edition.

9. Quoted in Earl A. Knies, The Art of Charlotte Brontë (Athens: Ohio University Press, 1969), p. 58.

10. Cf. Andrew D. Hook, "Charlotte Brontë, the Imagination and Villette," The Brontës: A Collection of Critical Essays, ed. Ian Gregor, Twentieth Century Views, (Englewood Cliffs, N.J.: Prentice Hall, Inc., 1970), p. 155: "Subjection to passionate feeling involves the temporary loss of individual identity."

11. Charlotte Brontë, The Professor (London: Smith, Elder and Co., 1905), pp. 231-32. All subsequent page references to the novel are to this edition.

12. Quoted in Knies, p. 94.

13. David Lodge, Language of Fiction, p. 114.

14. Charlotte Brontë, Jane Eyre (London: Smith, Elder and Co., 1906), p. 435. All subsequent page references to the novel are to this edition.

15. Allen, p. 218.

16. Quoted in Martin, p. 94.

17. Tillotson, pp. 259-60.

18. Richard Chase, "The Brontës: A Centennial Observance," The Kenyon Review 9 (Fall 1947): 487-506.

19. Chase calls it "a symbolic castration": "The faculty of vision, the analysts have shown, is often identified in the unconscious with the energy of sex. When Rochester had tried to make love to Jane, she had felt 'a fiery hand grasp at her vitals:' the hand, then must be cut off." Cf. Allen, p. 216: "Rochester's mutilation is the symbol of Jane's triumph in the battle of the sexes"; Moglen, p. 143: "He is devitalized;

the fire of his passion burnt to ash; the quick of his nature paralyzed."

20. Quoted in Winifred Gérin, *Charlotte Brontë: The Evolution of a Genius* (London: Oxford University Press, 1967), p. 391.

21. Gérin, p. 389.

22. Phyllis Bentley, *The Brontës* (London: Home and Van Thal, 1947), p. 74.

23. See, for example, Janet Spens, "Charlotte Brontë," *Essays and Studies* 14 (1929): 63-64; J.M.S. Tompkins, "Caroline Helstone's Eyes," *Brontë Society Transactions* 14 (1961): 21-22.

24. Martin, pp. 123-24.

25. See, for example, Martin, p. 128. Even Spacks, pp. 69-70, takes these comments by Shirley as consistent with her other characteristics.

26. Martin, pp. 139-40.

27. Margaret Lane, Introduction *Villette*, by Charlotte Brontë (London: J.M. Dent and Sons Ltd., 1909), p. vi.

28. Her name, of course, suggests coldness. Martin, pp. 149-50, quotes a comment made by Charlotte Brontë to W.W. Williams: "A *cold* name she must have partly, perhaps, on the '*lucus a non lucendo*' principle—partly on that of the 'fitness of things', for she has about her an external coldness." At one point Charlotte Brontë was to have called Lucy Miss Frost.

29. Hook, p. 154. Moglen points out that "in her letters to Ellen Nussey, Charlotte uses the word 'imagination' as a euphemism for sexual fantasy," p. 111.

30. Charlotte Brontë, *Villette* (London: Smith, Elder & Co., 1905), p. 35. All subsequent page references to this novel are to this edition.

31. Martin quotes Mrs. Gaskell as saying that Charlotte Brontë's father requested a happy ending for *Villette*, but Charlotte had always imagined Monsieur Paul dying at sea and refused to abandon her original conception, p. 186. Millett's discussion of *Villette*, pp. 139-47, one of the earliest and most challenging feminist treatments of the novel, surely overstates the feminist significance of this ending. Cf. Carolyn V. Platt, "How Feminist is *Villette*?" *Women and Literature*, 3 (Spring 1975): 16-27.

Chapter Five

1. One could argue for including *Romola* (1862-63) but, although Savonarola performs some of the functions of the right suitor, he is not one. The setting in fifteenth-century Florence also presents problems in considering Romola as a nineteenth-century heroine. *Felix Holt* was discussed in chapter two.

2. Most critics agree on this. See, for example, Bernard J. Paris, *Experiments in Life: George Eliot's Quest for Values* (Detroit: Wayne State University Press, 1965), p. 129.
3. John Holloway, *The Victorian Sage* (1953; rpt. New York: W.W. Norton and Co. Inc., 1965), p. 111.
4. Quoted by Basil Willey, *Nineteenth Century Studies: Coleridge to Matthew Arnold* (1949; rpt. New York: Harper and Row, 1966), p. 244.
5. George Eliot, *The Mill on the Floss*, ed. Gordon S. Haight (Boston: Houghton Mifflin Co., 1961), p. 435. All subsequent references to the novel are to this edition.
6. Quoted by Barbara Hardy, *The Novels of George Eliot: A Study in Form* (1959; rpt. New York: Oxford University Press, 1967), p. 16.
7. George Eliot, *Adam Bede* (New York: Harcourt, Brace and World, Inc., 1962), p. 170. All subsequent page references to the novel are to this edition.
8. Paris, p. 59. Cf. Calvin Bedient, *Architects of the Self: George Eliot, D. H. Lawrence, and E. M. Forster* (Berkeley and Los Angeles: University of California Press, 1972), p. 34: "For her [George Eliot] any society is preferably to the explosive egoism of the individual." Cf. Carol Christ, "Aggression and Providential Death in George Eliot's Fiction," *Novel* 9 (Winter 1976): 130-40. Kathleen Blake, *Middlemarch* and The Woman Question," *Nineteenth-Century Fiction* 31, (December 1976): 285-312, makes an interesting argument to support the idea that "For all her criticism of the shabby devices of egoism, Eliot never suggests that there is any way of transcending it."
9. Willey, p. 250.
10. Joan Bennett, *George Eliot: Her Mind and Her Art.* (1948; rpt. Cambridge: Cambridge University Press, 1962), p. 4.
11. Henry James, "George Eliot's *Middlemarch,*" *Galaxy* 15 (March 1873): 424-28.
12. Barbara Hardy, p. 53. Cf. Paris, p. 100. Françoise Basch, *Relative Creatures: Victorian Women in Society and the Novel* (New York: Schocken Books, 1974), p. 251ff. outlines the critical debate over Hetty Sorrel as a tragic figure.
13. See, for example, Paris, p. 118 and Darrell Mansell, Jr., "George Eliot's Conception of 'Form,'" *Studies in English Literature* 5 (Fall 1965): 651-62.
14. Jerome Thale, *The Novels of George Eliot* (New York: Columbia University Press, 1959), p. 146.
15. Barbara Hardy, pp. 26, 33. Paris, p. 154.
16. Barbara Hardy, p. 33: Adam "is some degrees removed from the Noble Savage, but provides something of the ironical rebuke which the Noble Savage makes to those who are more sophisticated but less noble."
17. Holloway, p. 132.
18. U.C. Knoepflmacher, "George Eliot, Feuerbach and the Question of Criticism," *Victorian Studies* 71 (March 1964): 306-309.

19. Barbara Hardy, p. 37.
20. Walter Allen, *The English Novel*, p. 263 claims that while there is criticism of Maggie in the novel, it is merely intellectual. F.R. Leavis, *The Great Tradition* (1945; rpt. New York: New York University Press, 1964), p. 41 says the soulful side of Maggie is offered with a remarkable absence of criticism.
21. Barbara Hardy, p. 55.
22. Gordon Haight, introduction to *The Mill on the Floss*, p. xv.
23. Barbara Hardy, p. 54.
24. Bennett, p. 119.
25. Haight, *Mill*, p. xi.
26. Leavis, *The Great Tradition*, pp. 43-44.
27. Bennett, p. 117, suggests rightly that there is some later improvement in Stephen under the influence of his love for Maggie.
28. Haight, *Mill*, p. xvi.
29. Ibid., p. xviii. See the discussion between Stephen and Maggie, pp. 393-94, 417; " . . . a superannuated blue-bottle which was exposing its imbecility in the spring sunshine, clearly against the views of Nature, who had provided Tom and the peas for the speedy destruction of this weak individual" (p. 78). Cf. Paris, p. 164.
30. Barbara Hardy, p. 52.
31. George Eliot, *Middlemarch*, ed. Gordon Haight (Boston: Houghton Mifflin Co., 1956), p. 16. All subsequent page references to the novel are to this edition. See Blake, p. 289 for a fuller discussion of this point.
32. Paris, p. 180. A passage from the ending in the first edition, later deleted by George Eliot, emphasizes this point: " . . . such mistakes could not have happened if the society into which she was born had not smiled on propositions of marriage from a sickly man to a girl less than half his own age—on modes of education which makes a woman's knowledge another name for motley ignorance—on rules of conduct which are in flat contradiction with its own loudly asserted beliefs" (p. 612).
33. Barbara Hardy, p. 164.
34. Henry James, "George Eliot's *Middlemarch*," cf. Allen, p. 272.
35. Thale, p. 119.
36. U.C. Knoepflmacher, *Laughter and Despair: Readings in Ten Novels of the Victorian Era* (Berkeley and Los Angeles: University of California Press, 1971), p. 172. Cf. Bennett, p. 176.
37. Barbara Hardy, p. 222. Frederick Karl calls Will "a savior rather than a lover . . . mythical not realistic," (*A Reader's Guide to the Nineteenth Century British Novel*, p. 288).
38. George Eliot, *Daniel Deronda*, intro. F.R. Leavis (New York: Harper and Row, 1961), p. 25. All subsequent page references to the novel are to this edition.
39. Thale, p. 126.

40. Edmund Dowden, "Middlemarch and Daniel Deronda," Contemporary Review 29 (February 1877): 348-69.
41. Thale, p. 123.
42. Ibid. p. 129. He also relates Gwendolen's fear of sexuality to her general desire for dominance.
43. Barbara Hardy, p. 154. Cf. Patricia Meyer, The Female Imagination, pp. 47-54.
44. Henry James, "Felix Holt, The Radical," Nation, 16 August 1866, pp. 127-28.

Chapter Six

1. E.M. Forster, A Room with a View (New York: Vintage-Knopf, n.d.), p. 47. All subsequent page references to the novel are to this edition.
2. Frederick Karl, A Reader's Guide to the Nineteenth Century British Novel, p. 231.
3. Dorothy Van Ghent, The English Novel, p. 223. Cf. Karl, p. 224.
4. Karl, p. 23.
5. Gillian Beer, Meredith: A Change of Masks (London: The Athlone Press, 1970) p. 128.
6. Ibid., p. 131.
7. Walter F. Wright, Art and Substance in George Meredith: A Study in Narrative (Loncoln: University of Nebraska Press, 1953), p. 73.
8. George Meredith, The Egoist (New York: Signet, 1963), p. 13. All subsequent page references to the novel are to this edition. The Egoist, Ann Veronica, and The Odd Women are all discussed in the penultimate chapter of Jenni Calder's Women and Marriage in Victorian Fiction.
9. John Goode, "The Egoist: Anatomy or Striptease?" in Meredith Now: Some Critical Essays, ed. Ian Fletcher (New York: Barnes and Noble, 1971), p. 219.
10. Karl, p. 218.
11. Angus Wilson, Afterward to The Egoist, p. 506.
12. Goode, p. 223. Kate Millett Sexual Politics, p. 139, also points out the antifeminism implicit in the marriage to Whitford.
13. E.M. Forster, "A View without a Room: Old Friends Fifty Years Later," The New York Times Book Review, 27 July 1958, p. 4.
14. Calvin Bedient, Architects of the Self, p. 192.
15. Forster, "A View without a Room."
16. Bedient, p. 202.
17. Wilfred Stone, The Cave and the Mountain: A Study of E.M. Forster (Stanford: Stanford University Press, 1966), p. 222.

18. Patrick Parrinder, ed., *H.G. Wells: The Critical Heritage* (London: Routledge and Kegan Paul, 1972), p. 173.

19. H.G. Wells, *Ann Veronica* (London: J.M. Dent and Sons Ltd., 1943), p. 5. All subsequent page references to the novel are to this edition.

20. George Gissing, *The Odd Women* (New York: Stein and Day, 1968), p. 37. All subsequent page references to the novel are to this edition.

Conclusion

1. E.M. Forster, "A View Without a Room," p. 4.

2. Doris Lessing, *The Summer Before the Dark* (New York: Bantam, 1974), p. 244.

3. Patricia Meyer Spacks, *The Female Imagination*, p. 369, has an interesting discussion on the use of hair in *The Summer Before the Dark*.

4. Erica Jong, *Fear of Flying* (New York: Signet, 1974), p. 10. All subsequent page references to the novel are to this edition.

5. Norma Rosen, "Who's Afraid of Erica Jong," *The New York Times Magazine*, 28 July 1974, p. 8.

6. Adrienne Rich, "When We Dead Awaken: Writing As Revision," *College English* 34, no. 1 (October 1972): 18-25.

7. Virginia Woolf, *A Room of One's Own* (1929; rpt. New York: Harcourt, Brace and World, Inc., 1957), p. 86.

8. Elizabeth Fishel, "End of the Waltz: The Rise of the Feminist Novel," *Human Behavior*, June 1976, pp. 64-69.

Selected Bibliography

The bibliography is limited to those works which have influenced this study. Inclusion does not necessarily indicate a feminist approach.

I. General

Books:

ALLEN, Walter. *The English Novel: A Short Critical History.* New York: E.P. Dutton and Co., 1954.

BASCH, Françoise. *Relative Creatures: Victorian Women in Society and the Novel.* New York: Schocken Books, 1974.

BEER, Patricia. *Reader, I Married Him: A Study of the Women Characters in Jane Austen, Charlotte Brontë, Elizabeth Gaskell and George Eliot.* New York: Barnes and Noble, 1974.

CALDER, Jenni. *Women and Marriage in Victorian Fiction.* New York: Oxford University Press, 1976.

CECIL, David. *Victorian Novelists: Essays in Revaluation.* Chicago: University of Chicago Press, 1958.

COLBY, Vineta. *The Singular Anomaly: Women Novelists of the Nineteenth Century.* New York: New York University Press, 1970.

——————. *Yesterday's Woman: Domestic Realism in the English Novel.* Princeton: Princeton University Press, 1974.

CORNILLON, Susan Koppelman, ed. *Images of Women in Fiction: Feminist Perspectives.* Bowling Green University Press, 1972.

DIAMOND, Arlyn and Lee Edwards, eds. *The Anatomy of Experience: Essays in Feminist Criticism.* Amherst: University of Massachusetts Press, 1977.

DONOVAN, Josephine, ed. *Feminist Literary Criticism: Explorations in Theory.* Lexington: University of Kentucky Press, 1975.

ELLMAN, Mary. *Thinking About Women.* New York: Harcourt, Brace and World, 1968.

FERGUSON, Mary Anne, ed. *Images of Women in Literature.* New York: Houghton Mifflin, 1973.

GREER, Germaine. *The Female Eunuch.* New York: McGraw-Hill, 1970.

HARDWICK, Elizabeth. *Seduction and Betrayal: Women and Literature.* New York: Random House, 1974.

HEILBRUN, Carolyn. *Toward a Recognition of Androgyny.* New York: Harper and Row, 1973.

KAPLAN, Sydney Janet. *Feminine Consciousness in the Modern British Novel.* Urbana: University of Illinois Press, 1975.

KARL, Frederick. *A Reader's Guide to the Nineteenth Century British Novel.* New York: The Noonday Press, 1964.

KETTLE, Arnold. *An Introduction to the English Novel.* New York: Harper and Row, 1968.

KNOEPFLMACHER, U. C. *Laughter and Despair: Readings in Ten Novels of the Victorian Era.* Berkeley and Los Angeles: University of California Press, 1971.

LEAVIS, F. R. *The Great Tradition.* New York: New York University Press, 1945.

MEWS, Hazel. *Frail Vessels: Woman's Role in Women's Novels From Fanny Burney to George Eliot.* London: The Athlone Press, 1969.

MILLETT, Kate. *Sexual Politics.* New York: Equinox, 1970.

MOERS, Ellen. *Literary Women: The Great Writers.* New York: Doubleday and Co., 1976.

RICH, Adrienne. *Of Woman Born: Motherhood as Experience and Institution.* New York: W.W. Norton and Co., Inc., 1976.

SHOWALTER, Elaine. *A Literature of their Own: British Woman Novelists from Brontë to Lessing.* Princeton: Princeton University Press, 1977.
SPACKS, Patricia Meyer. *The Female Imagination.* New York: Alfred A Knopf, 1975.
THOMPSON, Patricia. *The Victorian Heroine: A Changing Ideal, 1837-73.* London: Oxford University Press, 1956.
TILLOTSON, Kathleen. *Novels of the Eighteen-Forties.* London: Oxford University Press, 1961.
VICINUS, Martha, ed. *Suffer and Be Still: Women in the Victorian Age.* Bloomington: Indiana University Press, 1972.
WILLEY, Basil. *Nineteenth Century Studies: Coleridge to Matthew Arnold.* New York: Harper and Row, 1949.

Articles:

FERRIER, Carole. "Notes Toward a Feminist Criticism." *Hecate* 2, no. 1 (1976): 92-96.
FISHEL, Elizabeth. "End of the Waltz: The Rise of the Feminist Novel." *Human Behavior,* June 1976, pp. 64-69.
GORKY, Susan. "Old Maids and New Women: Alternatives to Marriage in Englishwomen's Novels, 1847-1915." *Journal of Popular Culture* 7 (1973): 68-85.
KAPLAN, Ann. "Feminist Criticism: A Survey with an Analysis of Methodological Problems." *University of Michigan Papers in Women's Studies* 1, no. 1 (1974): 150-77.
KOLODNY, Annette. "Some Notes on Defining a 'Feminist Literature.'" *Critical Inquiry* 2 (August 1975): 75-92.
PRATT, Annis. "The New Feminist Criticism." *College English* 32 (May 1971): 877.
————. "Archetypal Approaches to the New Feminist Criticism." *Bucknell Review* 21 (Spring 1973): 3-14.
RICH, Adrienne. "When We Dead Awaken: Writing as Revision." *College English* 34, no. 1 (October 1972): 18-25.
ROSEN, Norma. "Who's Afraid of Erica Jong?" *The New York Times Magazine,* 28 July 1974, p. 8.

SUDRANN, Jean. "Hearth and Horizon: Changing Concepts of the Domestic Life of the Heroine." *The Massachusetts Review* 14 (Spring 1973): 235-55.
YEAZELL, Ruth. "Fictional Heroines and Feminist Critics." *Novel* 8 (Fall 1974): 29-38.

II. Jane Austen

Books:

BRADBROOK, Frank. *Jane Austen and Her Predecessors.* Cambridge: Cambridge University Press, 1966.
BROWER, Reuben. *The Fields of Light: An Experiment in Critical Reading.* New York: Oxford University Press, 1951.
BUTLER, Marilyn. *Jane Austen and the War of the Ideas.* Oxford: Clarendon Press, 1975.
HALPERIN, John, ed. *Jane Austen: Bicentenary Essays.* New York: Cambridge University Press, 1975.
HARMSEL, Henrietta ten. *Jane Austen: A Study in Fictional Conventions.* The Hague: Mouton, 1964.
LITZ, A. Walton. *Jane Austen: A Study of Her Artistic Development.* New York: Oxford University Press, 1965.
MOLER, Kenneth. *Jane Austen's Art of Allusion.* Lincoln: University of Nebraska Press, 1968.
MUDRICK, Marvin. *Jane Austen: Irony or Defense and Discovery.* Princeton: Princeton University Press, 1952.
TAVE, Stuart. *Words of Jane Austen.* Chicago: University of Chicago Press, 1973.
WRIGHT, Andrew. *Jane Austen's Novels: A Study in Structure.* London: Chatto andWindus, 1961.

Articles:

AMIS, Kingsley. "What Became of Jane Austen?" *The Spectator* 4 (October 1957): 339-40.
BERGER, Carole. "The Rake and the Reader in Jane Austen's Novels." *Studies in English Literature, 1500-1900* 15 (1975): 531-44.

BROWN, L. W. "Jane Austen and the Feminist Tradition." *Nineteenth-Century Fiction* 28 (December 1973): 321-38.

GUBAR, Susan. "Sane Jane and the Critics: 'Professions and Falsehoods.'" *Novel* 8 (1975): 246-59.

KINKEAD-WEEKES, Mark. "This Old Maid: Jane Austen Replies to Charlotte Brontë and D. H. Lawrence." *Nineteenth-Century Fiction* 30 (December 1975): 399-420.

KLINGER, Samuel. "Jane Austen's *Pride and Prejudice* in the Eighteenth Century Mode." *University of Toronto Quarterly* 16 (1947): 357-71.

MAGEE, William. "The Happy Marriage: The Influence of Charlotte Smith on Jane Austen." *Studies in the Novel* 7 (Spring 1975): 120-32.

MONAGHAN, David M. "The Decline of the Gentry: A Study of Jane Austen's Attitude to Formality in *Persuasion*." *Studies in the Novel* 7 (Spring 1975): 73-87.

MUNDAY, M. "Jane Austen, Women Writers and *Blackwood's Magazine*." *Notes and Queries* 20 (August 1973): 290.

SHAW, Valerie. "Jane Austen's Subdued Heroines." *Nineteenth-Century Fiction* 30 (December 1975): 281-303.

TANNER, Tony. Introduction to *Sense and Sensibility*. Baltimore: Penguin Books, 1969.

VAH GHENT, Dorothy. "Pride and Prejudice." In *The English Novel: Form and Function*. New York: Harper and Row, 1953: 123-138.

WILSON, Edmund. "A Long Talk About Jane Austen." In *Classics and Commericals: A Literary Chronicle of the Forties*. New York: Farrar, Straus and Cudahy, Inc., 1950: 196-203.

III. *Charlotte Brontë*

Books:

BENTLEY, Phyllis. *The Brontës*. London: Home and Van Thal, 1947.

DUTHIE, Enid. *The Foreign Vision of Charlotte Brontë*. New York: Barnes & Noble, 1975.

EUBANK, Inga-Stina. *Their Proper Sphere: A Study of the Brontë Sisters as Early Victorian Female Novelists.* Cambridge: Harvard University Press, 1968.

GÉRIN, Winifred. *Charlotte Brontë: The Evolution of a Genius.* London: Oxford University Press, 1967.

GREGOR, Ian, ed. *The Brontës: A Collection of Critical Essays.* Englewood Cliffs, N.J.: Prentice Hall, Inc., 1970.

KNIES, Earl. *The Art of Charlotte Brontë.* Athens: Ohio University Press, 1969.

MARTIN, Robert. *Charlotte Brontë's Novels: The Accents of Persuasion.* New York: W.W. Norton and Co., Inc., 1968.

MOGLEN, Helen. *Charlotte Brontë: The Self-Conceived.* New York: W. W. Norton & Co., Inc., 1976.

PETERS, Margot. *Charlotte Bronte: Style in the Novel.* Madison: University of Wisconsin Press, 1974.

_____. *Unquiet Soul: The Biography of Charlotte Brontë.* Garden City, N.Y.: Doubleday and Co., 1975.

WILKS, Brian. *The Brontës.* New York: Viking Press, 1975.

Articles:

BLOM, M. A. "Charlotte Brontë: Feminist Manqué." *Bucknell Review* 21 (Spring 1973): 87-102.

_____. "Jane Eyre: Mind as Law Unto Itself." *Criticism* 15 (Fall 1973): 350-64.

BUCKHART, Charles. "The Nuns of Villette." *Victorian Newsletter* 44 (1973): 8-13.

CHASE, Richard. "The Brontës: A Centennial Observance." *The Kenyon Review* 9 (Fall 1947): 487-506.

HOGAN, J. "Enemies of Freedom in Jane Eyre." *Criticism* 13 (Fall 1971): 351-76.

PLATT, Carolyn V. "How Feminist is *Villette*?" *Women and Literature* 3 (Spring 1975): 16-27.

RICH, Adrienne. "Jane Eyre: The Temptations of a Motherless Woman." *Ms* 2 (October 1973): 68-72.

SPENS, Janet. "Charlotte Brontë." *Essays and Studies* 14 (1929): 63-64.

TOMPKINS, J.M.S. "Caroline Helstone's Eyes." *Brontë Society Society Transactions* 14 (1961): 21-22.

IV. *Emily Brontë*

DINGLE, Herbert. *The Mind of Emily Brontë.* London: Martin, Brian & O'Keefe, 1974.

CRANDALL, Norma. *Emily Brontë, A Psychological Portrait.* New York: Kraus Reprint Co., 1970.

VOLGER, Thomas, ed. *Twentieth-Century Interpretations of Wuthering Heights.* Englewood Cliffs, N.J.: Prentice Hall, Inc., 1968.

Articles:

BEVERSLUIS, John. "Love and Self-Knowledge: A Study of *Wuthering Heights.*" *English* 24 (1975): 77-82.

GRUDIN, Peter D. "*Wuthering Heights:* The Question of Unquiet Slumbers." *Studies in the Novel* 6 (1974): 389-407.

LEAVIS, Q. D. "A Fresh Approach to *Wuthering Heights.*" In *Lectures in America,* by F. R. And Q. D. Leavis. New York: Pantheon Books, 1969: 85-152.

OHMANN, Carol. "Emily Brontë in the Hands of Male Critics." *College English* 32 (May 1971): 906-13.

V. *Wilkie Collins*

Books:

MARSHALL, William. *Wilkie Collins.* New York: Twayne, Publishers, Inc., 1970.

ROBINSON, Kenneth. *Wilkie Collins: A Biography.* London: Davis-Poynter, 1974.

VI. George Eliot

Books:

BEDIENT, Calvin. *Architects of the Self: George Eliot, D. H. Lawrence, and E. M. Forster.* Berkeley: and Los Angeles: University of California Press, 1972.

BENNETT, Joan. *George Eliot: Her Mind and Her Art.* Cambridge: Cambridge University Press, 1962.

BONAPARTE, Felicia. *Will and Destiny: Morality and Tragedy in George Eliot's Novels.* New York: New York University Press, 1975.

HARDY, Barbara. *The Novels of George Eliot: A Study in Form.* New York: Oxford University Press, 1967.

PARIS, Bernard. *Experiments in Life: George Eliot's Quest for Values.* Detroit: Wayne State University Press, 1965.

REDINGER, Ruby. *George Eliot: The Emergent Self.* New York: Alfred A. Knopf, 1975.

ROBERTS, Neil. *George Eliot: Her Beliefs and Her Art.* Pittsburgh: University of Pittsburgh Press, 1975.

SMALLEY, Barbara. *George Eliot and Flaubert: Pioneers of the Modern Novel.* Athens: Ohio University Press, 1974.

THALE, Jerome. *The Novels of George Eliot.* New York: Columbia University Press, 1959.

Articles:

AUSTEN, Zelda. "Why Feminist Critics are Angry with George Eliot." *College English* 37 (February 1976): 549-61.

AUERBACH, Nina. "The Power of Hunger: Demonism and Maggie Tulliver." *Nineteenth-Century Fiction* 30 (September 1975): 150-71.

BLAKE, Kathleen. "*Middlemarch* and the Woman Question." *Nineteenth-Century Fiction* 31 (December 1976): 285-312.

CHRIST, Carol. "Aggression and Providential Death in George Eliot's Fiction." *Novel* 9 (Winter 1976): 130-40.

EDWARDS, Lee. "Women, Energy, and *Middlemarch.*" *Massachusetts Review* 13 (1972): 223-38.

FERNANDO, Lloyd. "George Eliot, Feminism, and Dorothea Brooke." *Review of English Literature* 4 (January 1963): 76-90.

————. "Special Pleading and Art in *Middlemarch:* The Relations Between the Sexes." *Modern Language Review* 67 (1972): 44-49.

HAIGHT, Gordon. Introduction to *Mill on the on the Floss.* Boston: Houghton Mifflin Co., 1961.

JAMES, Henry. "George Eliot's *Middlemarch.*" *Galaxy* 15 (March 1873): 424-28.

KNOEPFLMACHER, U. C. "George Eliot, Feuerbach and the Question of Criticism." *Victorian Studies* 71 (March 1964): 306-309.

MANSELL, Darrell, Jr. "George Eliot's Conception of 'Form.'" *Studies in English Literature* 5 (Fall 1965): 651-62.

VII. *E. M. Forster*

Books:

BRANDEN, Lawrence. *E. M. Forster: A Critical Study.* Lewisburg: Bucknell University Press, 1970.

COLMER, John. *E. M. Forster: The Personal Voice.* London: Rutledge, 1975.

FINKELSTEIN, Bonnie. *Forster's Women: Eternal Differences.* New York: Columbia University Press, 1975.

McDOWELL, Frederick. *E. M. Forster.* New York: Twayne Publishers, Inc., 1969.

STONE, Wilfred. *The Cave and the Mountain: A Study of E. M. Forster.* Stanford: Stanford University Press, 1966.

Articles:

BEER, John. "A Room with A View." *Times Literary Supplement,* 11 June 1971, p. 677.

FORSTER, E. M. "A View Without A Room: Old Friends Fifty Years Later." *The New York Times Book Review,* 27 July 1958, p. 4.

ELLEM, Elizabeth. "E. M. Forster: The Lucy and New Lucy Novels—Fragments of Early Versions of *A Room with A View.*" *Times Literary Supplement,* 28 May 1971, pp. 623-25.

VIII. *Elizabeth Gaskell*

CRAIK, Wendy. *Elizabeth Gaskell and the English Provincial Novel.* London: Methuen, 1975.
GANZ, Margaret. *Elizabeth Gaskell: The Artist in Conflict.* New York: Twayne Publishers, Inc., 1969.
LANSBURY Carol. *Elizabeth Gaskell: The Novel of Social Crisis.* London: Paul Elek, 1975.
MCVEAGH, John. *Elizabeth Gaskell.* New York: Humanities, 1970.

Articles:

SHELSTON, A. J. "*Ruth:* Mrs. Gaskell's Neglected Novel." *Bulletin of the John Rylands Library* 58 (1975): 173-92.
SMITH, David. "*Mary Barton* and *Hard Times:* Their Social Insights." *Mosaic* 5 (1972): 97-112.

IX. *George Gissing*

Books:

POOLE, Adrian. *Gissing in Context.* London: MacMillan, 1975.
SPIERS, John and Pierre Coustillas. *The Rediscovery of George Gissing.* London: National Book League, 1971.
TINDALL, Gillian. *The Born Exile: George Gissing.* London: Temple Smith, 1974.

X. *Thomas Hardy*

Books:

BROOKS, Jean. *Thomas Hardy: The Poetic Structure.* Ithaca: Cornell University Press, 1971.

GREGOR, Ian. *The Great Web: The Form of Hardy's Major Fiction.* Totowa, N.J.: Rowman and Littlefield, 1974.

GUERARD, Albert, ed. *Hardy: A Collection of Critical Essays.* Twentieth Century Views. Englewood Cliffs, N.J.: Prentice Hall, 1963.

HALLIDAY, F. E. *Thomas Hardy: His Life and Work.* Bath: Adams and Dart, 1972.

HORNBACH, Bert. *Metaphor of Chance: Vision and Technique in the Works of Thomas Hardy.* Athens: Ohio University Press, 1971.

KRAMER, Dale. *Thomas Hardy: The Forms of Tragedy.* Detroit: Wayne State University Press, 1974.

MEISEL, Perry. *Thomas Hardy: The Return of the Repressed— A Study of the Major Fiction.* New Haven: Yale University Press, 1972.

MILLER, J. Hillis. *Thomas Hardy: Distance and Desire.* Cambridge: Belknap, 1970.

SOUTHERINGTON, Frank. *Hardy's Vision of Man.* New York: Barnes and Noble, 1971.

VIGAR, Penelope. *The Novels of Thomas Hardy: Illusion and Reality.* London: Athlone, 1974.

Articles:

BENVENUTO, Richard. "*The Return of the Native* as a Tragedy in Six Books." *Nineteenth-Century Fiction* 26 (1971): 83-93.

EGGENSCHWILER, David. "Eustacia Vye, Queen of Night and Courtly Pretender." *Nineteenth-Century Fiction* 25 (1971): 444-54.

GRAY, Carole. "Jude and the 'New' Morality." *Christianity and Literature* 19 (1970): 14-21.

MARTIN, Bruce. "Whatever Happened to Eustacia Vye?" *Studies in the Novel* 4 (1972): 619-27.

ROGERS, Katherine. "Women in Thomas Hardy." *The Centennial Review* 19 (1975): 249-58.

192 / Victims of Convention

XI. George Meredith

Books:

BEER, Gillian. *Meredith: A Change of Masks*. London: The Athlone Press, 1970.

FLETCHER, Ian, ed. *Meredith Now: Some Critical Essays*. New York: Barnes and Noble, 1971.

WILT, Judith. *The Readable People of George Meredith*. Princeton: Princeton University Press, 1975.

WRIGHT, Walter. *Art and Substance in George Meredith: A Study in Narrative*. Lincoln: University of Nebraska Press, 1953.

Articles:

McCULLEN, M. L. "Handsome Heroes and Healthy Heroines: Patterns of the Ideal in George Meredith's Later Novels." *Cithara* 14 (1975): 95-105.

XII. H. G. Wells

Books:

BELLAMY, William. *The Novels of Wells, Bennett and Galsworthy, 1890-1910*. New York: Barnes and Noble, 1971.

BORRELLO, Alfred. *H. G. Wells: Author in Agony*. Carbondale: Southern Illinois University Press, 1972.

WILLIAMSON, Jack. *H. G. Wells: Critic of Progress*. Baltimore; Mirage, 1973.

Index

Allen, Walter, 82, 86
Amis, Kingsley, 34, 35
Atwood, Margaret, 164, 165, 166
Austen, Jane, 9, 11, 13, 20, 46, 48, 54, 59, 80, 85, 86, 100, 109, 137, 150; *Emma*, 12, 14, 21, 22, 23, 35-40, 41, 45, 46, 81; *Mansfield Park*, 21, 22, 34-35, 36, 46-47; *Northanger Abbey*, 12, 22, 23, 24-28, 30, 35, 36; *Persuasion*, 22, 23, 36, 40-44, 47; *Pride and Prejudice*, 12, 21, 22, 23, 31-34, 35, 36, 40, 41, 44, 46, 56, 137; *Sense and Sensibility*, 21, 22, 23, 28-31, 33, 34, 36, 43

Basch, Françoise, 10
Beer, Gillian, 137
Beer, Patricia, 9
Bennett, Joan, 119
Bentley, Phyllis, 93
Booth, Wayne, 39, 40
Bray, Charles, 109
Brontë, Charlotte, 9, 15, 16, 46, 81-83, 158; *Jane Eyre*, 11, 81, 82, 83, 85-93, 94, 100, 103, 106, 107; *The Professor*, 82, 83-85, 99, 106, 107; *Shirley*, 14, 16, 37, 51, 60, 81, 82, 83, 92-99, 100, 106, 107, 155; *Villette*, 9, 81, 83, 85, 99-107

Brontë, Emily, 9, 70; *Wuthering Heights*, 13, 63, 64, 66-69, 70, 114
Brown, Rita Mae, 165
Brown, Rosellen, 164
Browning, Elizabeth Barrett, 164

Calder, Jenni, 9, 18
Cecil, David, 54, 66, 81
Chopin, Kate, 159
Colby, Vineta, 9
Collins, Wilkie, *The Woman in White*, 13, 48, 56-61, 63, 96, 155
Craik, Mrs., 17

Darwin, Charles, 120
Dickens, Charles, 18, 48
Dowden, Edmund, 130
Dreiser, Theodore, 145

Eliot, George, 9, 15, 46, 158, 164; *Adam Bede*, 47, 108, 109, 111, 112-116, 135; *Daniel Deronda*, 12, 16, 47, 108, 111, 129-135; *Felix Holt*, 13, 47, 51-54, 61, 111, 135; *Middlemarch*, 11, 12, 14, 54, 80, 108, 110, 111, 117, 119, 121-129, 130, 135, 158; *The Mill on the Floss*, 65, 108, 109, 110, 111, 116-121, 123, 126, 135; *Romola*, 110

Feminism, 9, 76, 77, 88, 93, 95, 121, 122, 136, 149, 150, 151, 161, 163, 165; feminist criticism, 9-10; See also Women, Victorian attitudes to
Feuerbach, 108
Fishel, Elizabeth, 165
Forster, E.M., 136; Howards End, 141, 144; A Passage to India, 141; A Room With a View, 15, 20, 141-145, 147, 151, 153, 159

Ganz, Margaret, 49
Gaskell, Elizabeth, Mary Barton, 13, 47, 48-51, 57, 61, 63, 80, 92; Ruth, 64-66, 67, 69, 73
Gerin, Winifred, 92
Gissing, George, 158; The Emancipated, 151; In the Year of the Jubilee, 151; The Odd Women, 15, 19, 60, 136, 151-157; The Whirlpool, 151
Goode, John, 138, 141
Godwin, Gail, 18, 166
Gould, Lois, 165

Haight, Gordon, 120
Hardwick, Elizabeth, 9
Hardy, Barbara, 110, 111, 115, 117, 119, 121, 122
Hardy, Thomas, 69, 70; Jude the Obscure, 9, 63, 64, 70, 71, 73, 76-79; The Return of the Native, 63, 70, 71-73, 75, 76; Tess of the D'Urbervilles, 63, 65, 69, 70, 71, 73-76, 79
Heroine, as every woman, 13, 24-25, 35, 46-61; death of, 46, 60, 63, 66, 67, 69, 73, 76, 117, 155; independence of, 13, 15, 34, 60-61, 83, 84, 90, 91, 92, 93, 95, 102, 106, 107, 110, 118, 128, 141, 144, 150, 152, 154, 155, 156; marriage of, 12, 14-16, 19, 22-24, 25, 28, 30, 33, 38-40, 53, 56, 59, 68, 75, 80, 84, 88, 116, 122, 124, 129, 132, 137, 148, 153,

161; maturity of, 11-15, 21, 22-23, 28, 34, 44, 46, 47, 51, 53, 60, 63, 70, 79, 80, 81, 85, 91, 93, 100, 106, 107, 110, 121, 128, 134, 136, 141, 146; See also Women, Victorian attitudes to
Holloway, John, 108, 115
Hook, Andrew, 101

James, Henry, 135, 145
Jong, Erica, Fear of Flying, 159, 161-163
Joyce, James, 145, 163

Karl, Frederick, 137, 140
Knoepflmacher, U.C., 115, 128

Lane, Margaret, 63, 100
Laurence, Margaret, 18, 164, 166
Lawrence, D.H., 19, 70, 77, 145, 158, 159
Leavis, F.R., 131
Leavis, Q.D., 68
Lennox, Charlotte, 12
Lesbianism, 37, 96-98, 166
Lessing, Doris, 19, 152, 163, 164, 166; The Summer Before the Dark, 159, 160-161
Lewes, George, 83, 116, 126
Litz, A. Walton, 21, 27, 31
Lodge, David, 75, 85

Martin, Robert, 95
Matriachal traditions, 164-165, 166
Meredith, George, 151; Diana of the Crossways, 137; The Egoist, 9, 12, 14, 15, 47, 136, 137-141, 142, 153
Mews, Hazel, 9
Miller, Isabel, 165
Millett, Kate, 9
Mill, John Stuart, 17, 18, 151
Moers, Ellen, 10
Moler, Kenneth, 22
Moore, Brian, 159
Mudrick, Marvin, 24, 34, 37, 40

Novel, gothic elements in, 24-28, 29, 85; as psychological allegory, 64, 67, 76; of sensibility, 11, 29; structure of, 10, 18, 20, 44, 92, 128, 141, 147, 159, 162, 166

Oates, Joyce Carol, 152, 160

Paris, Bernard, 109, 124
Pass, Gail, 165, 166
Piercy, Marge, 165

Radcliffe, Ann, 26
Reade, Charles, 16
Rich, Adrienne, 163, 164
Romanticism, 29, 81, 85, 86, 118, 120, 126
Rosen, Norma, 163
Ruskin, John, 16-17, 139, 153; See also Women, Victorian attitudes to

Sadleir, Michael, 56
Sarton, May, 165
Scott-James, R.A., 147
Showalter, Elaine, 10
Spacks, Patricia Meyer, 9
Steinberg, Michael, 74
Stephen, Leslie, 120
Stone, Wilfred, 144
Strachey, Joe St. Loe, 146
Suitors, convention of the two, 10-16, 18-20, 21-24, 30, 39, 40, 42, 44-45, 46-47, 49, 53, 56, 60, 61-62, 64, 67, 69, 71, 79, 80, 84, 86, 88, 97, 99, 100, 107, 108, 110, 112, 116, 121, 122, 126, 128, 134, 137, 141, 145, 146, 150, 157, 158-159, 160, 162, 163, 166; idealization of right, 14, 22, 38, 52-54, 86, 114, 128, 131, 134, 137; right as mentor, 14, 27, 38, 111, 119; right as commoner, 47, 50-51, 52, 55-56, 57-58, 114; wrong as aristocrat, 47, 50, 52, 55, 57, 58-59, 70, 112
Tanner, Tony, 21, 23
Thale, Jerome, 112, 129, 130
Thomson, Patricia, 9
Tillotson, Kathleen, 88
Trollope, Anthony, 15; *Dr. Thorne,* 13, 47-48, 54-56, 57, 61

Van Ghent, Dorothy, 22, 69
Ward, Mary A., 82
Wells, H.G., *Ann Veronica,* 15, 20, 136, 145-151, 153, 154
Willey, Basil, 110
Williams, W.S., 87, 92
Wilson, Angus, 141
Wilson, Edmund, 37, 40
Wollstonecraft, Mary, 17, 18
Women, Victorian attitudes to, 16-17, 60, 66, 79, 83, 123, 136, 147; See also Ruskin
Woolf, Virginia, 18, 108, 158, 165
Wright, Walker, 137